The

TOTAL MONEY

MAKEOVER

Other Books from Dave Ramsey

The Total Money Makeover Spanish Edition
(La Transformación Total de su Dinero)
ISBN 0-8811-3772-3

Financial Peace

Financial Peace Revisited

Financial Peace Planner

Financial Peace for the Next Generation
(Youth Book)

Tranquilidad Financiera
(Spanish edition of *Financial Peace*)

More Than Enough

More Than Enough Planner

The Super Red Racer
(Children's Book)

Priceless
(Four-Color Gift Book)

The

TOTAL MONEY MAKEOVER

A Proven Plan for Financial Fitness

Dave Ramsey

THOMAS NELSON PUBLISHERS®
Nashville

A Division of Thomas Nelson, Inc.
www.ThomasNelson.com

Published in Nashville, Tennessee, by Thomas Nelson, Inc.

Scripture quotations noted NKJV are from THE NEW KING JAMES VERSION, Copyright © 1979, 1980, 1982, Thomas Nelson, Inc., Publishers.

Scripture quotations noted CEV are from THE CONTEMPORARY ENGLISH VERSION, © 1995 by the American Bible Society. Used by permission.

Library of Congress Cataloging-in-Publication Data

Ramsey, Dave.
    The total money makeover : a proven plan for financial fitness / Dave Ramsey.
        p. cm.
    ISBN 0-7852-6326-8 (Hardcover)
    1. Finance, Personal. 2. Debt. I. Title.
HG179.R31563 2003
332.024'02—dc21   2003014115

Printed in the United States of America
03 04 05 06 07 QWM 6 5 4 3 2 1

To my beautiful wife, Sharon, who walked arm in arm with me through a Total Money Makeover—I love you, honey.

To the superstars all across America who have had the courage to face the person in the mirror, the culture, their family, and even their coworkers as they "Lived like no one else so later they could live like no one else." You who have courageously had a Total Money Makeover of the heart and wallet are the real superstars.

To the Dave Ramsey team and the Thomas Nelson team for tireless hours on this project to make this material available to everyone across this great land.

Contents

The Total Money Makeover Challenge

"As lost as a ball in tall weeds!" That is exactly how I felt. Although it was fifteen years ago, I can still taste the emotion as if it were yesterday. Out of control, lost, no sense of power, I felt dread creep across the room like the afternoon shadows on a cold winter's day. Sitting again at the kitchen table with too much month left at the end of the money, I was not having fun. This "adult" stuff where a wife looks to you to provide and kids expect to be fed and kept warm was not exactly working. I didn't feel like some powerful adult; instead, there was a little boy inside me who was very afraid—afraid of this month's bills, afraid of this month's mortgage, and absolutely terrified when I considered the future. How was I to send kids to college, retire, enjoy life, and not live at the edge of money worries?

The "Normal" American Family

It seemed every month I sat at that same table with the same worries, fears, and problems. I had too much debt, too little savings, and no sense of control over my life. No matter how hard I worked, it seemed I couldn't win. I was to forever be slave to some banker, to the government, and to the "needs" of my family. When Sharon and I "talked" about money, we ended up in a fight, leaving her feeling afraid and me feeling inadequate.

I had too much debt, too little savings, and no sense of control over my life.

The next car purchase, the next house, the kids' college—our entire future seemed out of reach.

I didn't need a get-rich-quick guy to pump me up or tell me to be positive. I didn't need a secret formula to riches. I wasn't afraid of hard work or sacrifice. I didn't want to "feel" my way into being "positive." I was positive of only one thing: I was sick and tired of being sick and tired. I was tired of sitting down to "do the bills" and having a heaviness come over me. The hopelessness was overwhelming. I felt like a gerbil in a wheel—run, run, run, no traction, no ground covered; maybe life was just a financial illusion. All the money came in, all the money went out, and only the names were changed to protect the innocent. I owe, I owe, so off to work I go. You know the drill and all the clichés that go with the drill.

Oh, some months everything seemed to work, and I thought maybe we were going to be okay. I could tell myself then, "Oh well, this is how everyone lives." Those times offered enough wiggle room that I could continue to lie to myself that we were making headway, but deep down, I knew we weren't.

I Did It My Way, and My Way Wasn't Working

ENOUGH! THIS STINKS! I finally decided that this nonplan wasn't working. If you have ever had any of those feelings, you are going to love this book, and, more important, you will love *your* Total Money Makeover.

Fifteen years ago, my wife, Sharon, and I went broke. We lost everything due to my stupidity in handling money, or not handling it, as the case may be. Hitting bottom and hitting it hard was the worst thing that ever happened to me and the best thing that ever happened to me.

We started with nothing, but by the time I was twenty-six years old, we held real estate worth over $4 million. I was good at real estate, but

Myths vs. Truth

Myth: I don't have time to work on a budget, retirement plan, or estate plan.

Truth: You don't have time not to.

I was better at borrowing money. Even though I had become a millionaire, I had built a house of cards. The short version of the story is that we went through financial hell and lost everything over a three-year period of time. We were sued, foreclosed on, and, finally, with a brand-new baby and a toddler, we were bankrupt. *Scared* doesn't begin to cover it. *Crushed* comes close, but we held on to each other and decided we needed a change.

So after losing everything, I went on a quest, a quest to find out how money really works, how I could get control of it, and how I could have confidence in handling it. I read everything I could get my hands on. I interviewed older rich people, people who made money and kept it. That quest led me to a really, really uncomfortable place—my mirror. I came to realize that my money problems, worries, and shortages largely began and ended with the person in my mirror. I realized also that if I could learn to manage the character I shaved with every morning, I could win at money. That quest, the one that ended with me staring at myself in the mirror, led me on a new journey over the last fifteen years: the journey of helping others, literally millions of others, take that same quest to the mirror. Live Events, Financial Peace University, *The Dave Ramsey Show* (talk radio), and the *New York Times* best-sellers *Financial Peace* and *More Than Enough* have enabled me to tell millions of Americans what I have learned—the hard way—about money.

The Big Challenge: Find a Mirror

I have a challenge for you. Are you ready to take on the guy or gal in your mirror? If you are, you are ready to win. I rediscovered God's and

Grandma's simple way of handling money. Wealth building isn't rocket science, which is a good thing for me (and probably you). Winning at money is 80 percent behavior and 20 percent head knowledge. What to do isn't the problem; doing it is. Most of us know what to do, but we just don't do it. If I can control the guy in the mirror, I can be skinny and rich. We will let other books work on the skinny, and I will help you with the rich part. No, there are no secrets, and yes, this will be very hard. Hey, if it were easy, every moron walking would be wealthy.

> Winning at money is 80 percent behavior and 20 percent head knowledge.

So my Total Money Makeover begins with a challenge. The challenge is you. You are the problem with your money. The financial channel or some tape sets aren't your answer; you are. You are the king of your future, and I have a plan. The Total Money Makeover plan isn't theory. It works every single time. It works because it is simple. It works because it gets to the heart of your money problems: you. It is based on a series of prices that must be paid to win. All winners pay a price to win. Some losers pay a price and never win, and that is usually because they didn't have the benefit of a proven plan for financial fitness.

Ordinary People

Tens of thousands of ordinary people have used the system in this book to get out of debt, regain control, and build wealth. I've scattered their stories throughout the book, and I've included several more at the back of the book. If at any point during your makeover you are tempted to quit or you just need a little encouragement, read one of these stories. These people have sacrificed for a short period of time so they will never have to sacrifice again.

SHOCKING STATS

90% of people in our culture buy things they can't afford.

If you are looking for a road map to get you home, you've found it. If you are looking for something easy or fast, you have the wrong book. If you are looking for a book to help you pass your CPA exam in the area of financial knowledge, you have the wrong book. If you are looking for a writer who has intricate academic theories (which don't work in the real world), you've got the wrong guy. I have many of the academic pedigrees, but I ended up broke. I have actually twice become a millionaire from nothing. The first time I was in my twenties, the money was in real estate, and I lost that due to my stupidity; the second time I was not yet forty, but I did the money thing right that time, and I am debt-free.

I often hear about broke finance professors who bemoan that I am way too simple, or as an e-mailer told me on *The Dave Ramsey Show* one day, "You are a one-trick pony." To those of you who say you have great but unexecuted plans, I say, "Prove it. I have." I like the way I've built wealth better than the way you haven't. You will meet people, educated and uneducated, throughout this book who have won, or begun to win, with money for the first time in their lives. The Total Money Makeover works!

The Total Money Makeover Motto

This plan works, but it will cost you. It will teach you to say new words, like "no." In short, your Total Money Makeover will be a personal money makeover where you learn this motto: IF YOU WILL LIVE LIKE NO ONE ELSE, LATER YOU CAN LIVE LIKE NO ONE ELSE. This is the motto of your Total Money Makeover. It's my way of reminding you that if you will make the sacrifices now that most people aren't willing to

Dum Math & Stupid Tax

A False Sense of Security

Some people want to buy a new car for the warranty. If you lose $17,000 of value over four years, on average you have paid too much for a warranty. You could have completely rebuilt the car twice for $17,000!

make, later on you will be able to live as those folks will never be able to live. You will notice the motto all through the book, even across the bottom of the pages. I'm sorry there isn't an easier path to feature in the motto, but the good thing about this one is that it works. You can repeat the motto to yourself as you pass up a purchase in order to hit your goals. When you work late and are tired, you can say the motto to yourself. Of course, this isn't a magic formula; I'm not into that. But it does remind you that you *will* win, and the payoff *will* be worth the cost.

Some of you are so immature that you are unwilling to delay pleasure for a greater result. I will show you exactly how to get the result you want, so the price you pay will not be in vain. I

> You *will* win, and the payoff *will* be worth the cost.

don't want to walk across hot coals because it is fun, but if I can be shown how a short, painful walk will do away with the lifetime of worry, frustration, stress, and fear that being constantly broke brings me, then bring on the hot coals.

I had started my own business the "American way" . . . on credit! As I struggled to find new accounts, my older accounts were holding my money 40 to 160 days, so by the time I finally got the money, I had already floated all the month's

expenses on my credit cards. Before I knew it, we were $78,000 in debt, not including the house. We were in way too deep. I decided to get a second job, working with my old employer on a job-to-job basis for roughly 30 to 60 hours a week.

We got really focused and intense. I worked about 80 to 100 or more hours a week for the next several months and started knocking out debts one at a time. We sold our house and used the money to pay off the home equity line of $11,000 and moved into another house. I worked every day of the week from 4:30 A.M. till 2:00 A.M. I would often work all through one night and go to work the next day, not sleeping until midnight the next night! As a result, we were able to send six-, seven-, eight-thousand-dollar checks to the credit-card companies. We sold our truck and bought an '88 Honda Civic for $1,800 cash, and it's still running perfectly today!

It took pure determination to spend less that year so we could pay off the debt that took two years to accumulate. The last check I wrote was to CitiBank for $5,411, and it was the happiest day my wife and I had seen in a long time!

I now have a normal workweek, seeing my wife and children in the evenings. I am so thankful to Dave Ramsey's Total Money Makeover plan for giving me the tools and inspiration to free my family from a bondage that grasped us so tightly around our necks. After years of making only $48,000 a year, with hard work we paid off $78,000 of debt in twelve months! I may have been an extreme case, but I am proof that if you really decide you want to be free, it doesn't take as long as you think. You, too, will be on your way to success!

Shad Peck
Plumber

My Promise to You

My promise to you is this: If you will follow the guidelines of this proven system of sacrifice and discipline, you can be debt-free, begin saving, and give as you've never given before. You will build wealth. I will also promise you that it is totally up to you. The Total Money Makeover isn't a magic formula to wealth. This system will not work unless you do, and then only to the degree of your intensity in implementing it. In the following pages, you will meet many individuals and families that have won many money victories but not one of them won until they won the battle with the guy in the mirror. Your situation isn't your spouse's fault (well, maybe, but we'll talk later), it isn't your parents' fault, it isn't your children's fault, and it isn't your friends' fault. IT IS YOUR FAULT!

Dave Rants ...

> Savings without a mission is garbage. Your money needs to work for you, not lie around.

My financial life began turning around when I took responsibility for it. People all across America have used these steps to become free, regain a sense of confidence and control, and build a future for their families. Please join me on a journey away from the young man I was, the one I described earlier who was racked with worry, fear, and guilt over money. Take this journey with me to your own Total Money Makeover, but remember, the first part of the quest is confronting the man in the mirror. That man in the mirror is your Total Money Makeover Challenge.

2

Denial:
I'm Not *That* out of Shape

Several years ago I realized I had let my body dissolve into flab. I had worked so hard for so many years that I had abandoned the care of my physical condition. The first step to getting into shape was to realize I needed to change my ways, but the second and equally important step was to identify the obstacles to getting there. What would stop me from getting into shape? Once I understood those obstacles, I began a process to lose weight, grow muscle, and become more fit. Your Total Money Makeover is the same. You need to realize there's a problem, but you must also see what could hinder your move toward financial fitness. The next few chapters will identify some major obstacles to YOUR Total Money Makeover.

> ## Myths vs. Truth
>
> **Myth:** Debt consolidation saves interest, and you have one smaller payment.
>
> **Truth:** Debt consolidation is dangerous because you treat only the symptom.

Look in the mirror. Take a long look. What do you see? Suck in that gut; hold up your chest, and really look at yourself. It doesn't matter how many angles or poses you take, the mirror is cruel. "Well, I'm really not *that* fat, maybe just a little flabby." My dad used to say that

9

90 percent of solving a problem is realizing there is one. Focused intensity, life-or-death intensity, is required for you to reset your money-spending patterns, and one of your biggest obstacles is DENIAL. The sad thing is that you can be financially mediocre in this country, financially flabby, and still be average. And if the truth be known, being average, normal, and financially flabby is pretty much okay by most folks' standards. This, however, is not a book for the wimpy among us. This is a book about winning, about really having something.

> Ninety percent of solving a problem is realizing there is one.

---

*W*ound very tight." That was the best way to describe me when I started listening to Dave Ramsey. I could fast-talk people into thinking I knew how to make money; but the bottom line was, I didn't have a clue. I was in total denial. Reality was sleepless nights because of "floating" checks in the mail to pay bills and having to run my check to the bank at lunch to cover them. I used credit cards like everyone does. I argued that it was a wise use of my money. After all, it helped me to stretch my paycheck—to the tune of 18 to 29 percent in interest!

Then I hit bottom. Frustration was at its peak, and I knew I was not in control. I had racked up $45,000 in credit-card debt alone!

By following The Total Money Makeover plan, I have reduced that to $24,000 in twenty-four months. That's an average extra $875 going to kill debt each month! I pay my bills on time now, no more bounced-check reports in the mail, and I sleep like a baby! It took my admitting that I wasn't in control of my money, that my money was controlling me. I thank God for finding out about Dave Ramsey and The Total Money Makeover. If you think you may be

on the verge of financial trouble or just need some guidance, do The
Total Money Makeover plan. You literally can't afford not to!

> Randolph and Linda England
> (both age 53)
> Wastewater Operator and
> Technician; Schoolteacher

Don't Wait to Have Denial Knocked out of You

For several years I have spoken about fifteen times a year to live audiences of two thousand to eight thousand people, teaching them the ideas in this book. After one live event where I spoke to four thousand people, Sara told me that her Total Money Makeover came only after life placed a call to her. She said she had heard me quote the *Wall Street Journal* as reporting that 70 percent of Americans live paycheck to paycheck, but she honestly thought she was in the 30 percent who were fine. She had financially struck a pose, and the pose was denial.

Dave Rants . . .

For your own good, for the good of your family and your future, grow a backbone. When something is wrong, stand up and say it is wrong, and don't back down.

With two sons from her previous marriage, Sara had just remarried and was happy and secure in her job, as was her husband, John. Their new life together seemed awesome. Their household combined income was about $75,000 per year, with the "normal" debts of a small student loan, a car loan, and "only" $5,000 on a credit card. With life under control and even going well, Sara and John decided their new family needed a new home, so the builder was selected and construction began. Somewhere deep inside there may have been uneasiness, but it was very deep. Finally the day came when the new home was complete. Everything was going to be fine now, the new family in the new home, the way it is "supposed" to be. In May they moved into the new home, complete with big new payments.

In September Sara's boss asked to see her in his office. She was excelling at work and braced herself for a big "atta, girl" followed by a nice bonus or raise. Instead, the boss explained her job was being eliminated. "Downsizing, you know," he said. Her life's work was cut from her—and $45,000 of their $75,000 income—with the boss's chilling words. Not only was her pride hurt and her career path cut short, a creeping terror grew deep down inside as she drove home to tell John. That night there were tears, fears, and the sudden stark realization that she and John were financially fat. Suddenly, Sara and her family were facing foreclosure on the house and repossession of the car. The basics of life had become precious.

> ### Dum Math & Stupid Tax
>
> **Washer & Dryer for Sale—$1,800!**
>
> Yes, that's correct, and you, too, can get this sweet deal. Just head on down to your local rent-to-own store.

Sara and John had listened to *The Dave Ramsey Show* on the radio, but they always thought someone else needed a Total Money Makeover. After all, they always held their stomachs in when standing in front of the mirror. The night after her layoff was the first night they looked in the financial mirror and saw fat people. The sight wasn't pretty—big house payments, fat car payments, large student loans, bloated credit cards, anorexic savings, and no budget. They saw fat people.

When you are physically fat it is hard to be in denial, because there is the ever-widening belt line. When you are financially fat, however, you can fake it and look good for a while. Your friends and family will participate in your fantasy/denial, which makes you believe you are doing just fine. One of the four major factors that keep people from winning in money by getting a Total Money Makeover is not realizing they need one. Sadly, some of the most dramatic Makeovers I've seen have been by people who had life smack them so hard they got the denial knocked out of them, like Sara. If life isn't smacking you around at the moment, you are actually in greater danger than Sara and John the night of the layoff. You are a real candidate for financial mediocrity or even a major crisis brought on by denial, and you have to see the need to make dramatic changes. If you are apathetic because everything seems "just fine," then you will be unwilling to make the huge changes needed to get huge results.

> You have to see the need to make dramatic changes.

Mmm . . . Frog Legs

Years ago, in a motivational seminar by the master, Zig Ziglar, I heard a story about how mediocrity will sneak up on you. The story goes that if you drop a frog into boiling water, he will sense the pain and immediately jump out. However, if you put a frog in room-temperature water, he will swim around happily, and as you gradually turn the water up to boiling, the frog will not sense the change. The frog is lured to his death by gradual change. We can lose our health, our fitness, and our wealth gradually, one day at a time. It might be a cliché, but that's because it is true: The enemy of "the best" is not "the worst." The enemy of "the best" is "just fine."

> ### SHOCKING STATS
>
> 80% of graduating college seniors have credit-card debt—before they even have a job!

We were doing just fine in our "glass house." Talk about denial! We could pay all the bills; we just didn't have anything left over to save for the future. I work in collections, so I know all the problems from being in over your head. I really began to see how fast people could get into financial ruin. I knew we were headed in the same direction as the people I was trying to collect from. The road to financial ruin is a fast track, we were definitely on it, and I knew we had to get off quickly!

We needed direction. We started The Total Money Makeover plan and got on the narrow road to Financial Peace. We'll have paid off $11,000 in eight months and are well on the road to debt FREEDOM! It's amazing how I had bought into the same problems and denial I faced every day on the phone. I'm glad we saw the exit before we traveled too far.

Everyone needs The Total Money Makeover, not just those who are in over their heads. If you're not paying cash, you're paying too much. The Total Money Makeover plan gives hope not only to those who are hopeless; but it can give hope also to anyone who makes money. We all need direction on our financial road. So quit denying it!

> *Kathy (age 47)*
> *and James (age 49) Smith*
> *Asset Recovery Officer;*
> *Maintenance Technician*

The Pain of Change

Change is painful. Few people have the courage to seek out change. Most people won't change until the pain of where they are exceeds the pain of change. When it comes to money, we can be like the toddler in a soiled diaper. "I know it smells bad, but it's warm and it's mine." Only when the rash comes will we cry out. I hope Sara's story and the others in this book will make you unwilling to stay where you are. If you keep doing the same things, you will keep getting the same results. You are where you are right now financially as a sum total of the decisions you've made to this point. If you like where you are, keep it up. Keep in mind, however, why you are reading a book called *The Total Money Makeover*. Is it because deep down you have the same uneasy feeling Sara had but didn't address until it was almost too late? Are you really looking for something more? If so, I've got great news. This plan works! Break through the temptation to remain in the same situation, and opt for the pain of change before the pain of not changing searches you out. Don't wait for a heart attack to show you that you are overweight. Cut the carbs, the fats, the sugars, and lace up the running shoes now.

The good news about Sara and John was that the financial heart attack they had made them address their financial eating and exercise habits. The layoff was a wake-up call and the end to denial. After a year of very hard times, Sara was able to find a whole new career. Only this time when the checks started rolling in, Sara and John were using this system. Every paycheck became an exciting event because they had a plan. They were financially losing weight and toning up. It wasn't a quick process, but after following the steps over time, today they are really winning.

> Few people have the courage to seek out change.

The night I met Sara and John, they were two years into their plan—and smiling. They told me they were debt-free except for their house, and they had $12,000 in the bank just for emergencies. They had broken through their own denial, but they made their family uncomfortable because they refused to live like everyone else. Albert Einstein said, "Great spirits have always found violent opposition from mediocre minds." John's dad had made fun of their plan and the extra jobs they took to win. He asked if they had joined some cult or something. Once Sara and John had realized they were the emperor with no clothes, denial was no longer an option. They also realized all they had been doing with money to impress others—but no more.

Sara chuckled as she told me how she used to think: "We must be doing well; all these credit-card companies think I'm creditworthy." "If I'm getting approvals from all these banks, I must be okay because, otherwise, they wouldn't want to loan me money." "Besides, I pay my credit cards off every month. How could I be in any trouble?" "I can afford to buy that car or that furniture if I can afford the payment." John was grinning now, too, as they both laughed at the language of financially fat people who think they are fine, the language of denial.

As we closed our conversation that night, Sara told me that while she hoped she or John never lost another job unexpectedly, they are ready if they do. "We are no longer living a lie. We know where we are, we know where we are going, and we know how we are going to get there," she said. She and John wanted to leave me a gift for inspiring their Total Money Makeover, but I assured them they already had.

3

Debt Myths:
Debt Is (Not) a Tool

Red-faced and fists clenched, the toddler yells with murder in his voice, "I want it! I want it! I want it!" We have all watched this scene unfold in the grocery store. We may even have watched our own children do this (once). Now that I'm older and more mellow, I sometimes grin a little as a young mom tries without success to stifle the out-of-control screams of a child who is denied something.

> It is human nature to want it and want it now; it is also a sign of immaturity.

It is human nature to want it and want it now; it is also a sign of immaturity. Being willing to delay pleasure for a greater result is a sign of maturity. However, our culture teaches us to live for the now. "I want it!" we scream, and we can get it, if we are willing to go into debt. Debt is a means to obtain the "I want its" before we can afford them.

Joining in the Lie

I have heard it said that if you tell a lie often enough, loudly enough, and long enough, the myth will become accepted as a fact. Repetition, volume, and longevity will twist and turn a myth, or a lie, into a commonly accepted way of doing things. Entire populations have been lulled into the approval of ghastly deeds and even participation in them by gradually moving from the truth to a lie. Throughout history, twisted logic, rationalization, and incremental changes have allowed normally intelligent people to be party to ridiculous things. Propaganda, in particular, played a big part in allowing these things to happen.

Dum Math & Stupid Tax

**Freedom 15 Years Early
for About $250 a Month**

Imagine you buy a $130,000 home, for which you take out a $110,000 mortgage at 7%. The final cost after all is said and done and paid would be $283,520 after 30 years or $197,840 after 15. The difference? Just $256 extra per month. Go with 15 years!

We have propaganda in our culture today. I'm not speaking in a political sense, but rather recognizing that there are people out there who want us to think their way and who will go to great lengths to accomplish that. The financial and banking industries, in particular, are very good at teaching us their way of handling money, which of course leads us to buy their products. If I see an ad again and again that tells me I will be cool and sharp looking if I drive a certain car, I can fall under the illusion that with the purchase of that car, those good things will happen to me. We may not really believe that we will become a model just from purchasing a car, but notice that ugly people aren't used in the TV spots to sell cars. We aren't really falling for that lie, or are we? I'm just asking. After all, we do buy the car and then justify our purchase on the basis of something academic like gas mileage.

When we participate in what the crowd identifies as normal, even if it is stupid, we gain acceptance into the club. Sometimes we don't even realize what we are doing is stupid because we have been taught that it's just "the way you do it," and so we never ask why. As we participate in the myth, we learn to spout the principles of the myth. After the years go by and we have invested more money and time into the myth, we become great disciples and can preach the points of the myth with great fervor and volume. We become such experts on the myth that we can sell others on joining the lie. I once joined in the lie, but no more.

Don't Let the Monkeys Pull You Down!

Debt has been sold to us so aggressively, so loudly, and so often that to imagine living without debt requires myth-busting. We have to systematically destroy the inner workings of the myths. Debt is so ingrained into our culture that most Americans can't even envision a car without a payment, a house without a mortgage, a student without a loan, and credit without a card. We have been sold debt with such repetition and with such fervor that most folks cannot conceive what it would be like to have no payments. Just as slaves born into slavery can't visualize freedom, we Americans don't know what it would be like to wake up to no debt. Last year 5.3 billion credit-card offers were put in our mailboxes, and we are taking advantage of those offers. According to CardTrak, Americans currently have $660 billion in credit-card debt. We can't do without debt, or can we?

Working with tens of thousands of people on their Total Money Makeover in the last several years, I have found that a major barrier to winning is our view of debt. Most people who have made the decision to stop borrowing money have

A major barrier to winning is our view of debt.

experienced something weird: ridicule. Friends and family who are disciples of the myth that debt is good have ridiculed those on the path to freedom.

John Maxwell tells of a study done on monkeys. A group of monkeys were locked in a room with a pole at the center. Some luscious, ripe bananas were placed on top of the pole. When a monkey would begin to climb the pole, the experimenters would knock him off with a blast of water from a fire hose. Each time a monkey would climb, off he would go, until all the monkeys had been knocked off repeatedly, thus learning that the climb was hopeless. The experimenters then observed that the other primates would pull down any monkey trying to climb. They replaced a single monkey with one who didn't know the system. As soon as the new guy tried to climb, the others would pull him down and punish him for trying. One by one, each monkey was replaced and the scene repeated until there were no monkeys left in the room that had experienced the fire hose. Still, none of the new guys were allowed to climb. The other monkeys pulled them down. Not one monkey in the room knew why, but none were allowed to get the bananas.

We aren't monkeys, but sometimes we exhibit behavior that seems rather chimplike. We don't even remember why, we just know that debt is needed to win. So when a loved one decides to get a Total Money Makeover, we laugh, get angry, and pull him down. We Americans are like the last set of monkeys. With rolled eyes we spout the pat lines associated with the myth as if anyone not wanting to have debt is unintelligent. That person must be a simpleton, a fanatic, or, worst of all, "uneducated in finance." Then why are so many finance professors broke? I think a broke finance professor is like a shop teacher with missing fingers.

Myth vs. Truth

I want to expose the inner workings of the Debt Myth by looking at many of the sub-myths. However, I need to warn you to watch out for your instinct to defend the American way of borrowing. Calm down. Relax and go for a ride with me for a few pages. I might be onto something. If, at the end of this myth-busting section, you conclude I'm just a nut with a book, you will not be forced to change. But just in case the tens of thousands of families who have experienced a Total Money

Makeover have something to say to you, read on in a relaxed state. Let your guard down. You can always put the shields back up later.

Myth: **Debt is a tool and should be used to create prosperity.**

Truth: **Debt adds considerable risk, most often doesn't bring prosperity, and isn't used by wealthy people nearly as much as we are led to believe.**

When training for my first career in real estate, I remember being told that debt was a tool. "Debt is like a fulcrum and lever," allowing us to lift what we otherwise could not. We can buy a home, a car, start a business, or go out to eat and not be bothered with having to wait. I remember a finance professor telling us that debt was a two-edged sword, which could cut for you like a tool but could also cut into you and bring harm. The myth has been sold that we should use OPM, other people's money, to prosper. The academic garbage is spread really thick on this issue. We are told with sufficient snobbery and noses in the air that sophisticated and disciplined financiers use debt to their advantage. Careful there, you'll get a sunburn on your upper lip.

My contention is that debt brings on enough risk to offset any advantage that could be gained through leverage of debt. Given time, a lifetime, risk will destroy the perceived returns purported by the mythsayers.

> Debt brings on enough risk to offset any advantage that could be gained through leverage of debt.

I once was a mythsayer myself and could repeat the myths very convincingly. I was especially good with the "debt is a tool" myth. I have even sold rental property that was losing money to investors by showing them, with very sophisticated internal rates of return, how they would actually make money. Boy, what a reach. I could spout the myth with enthusiasm, but life and God had some lessons to teach me. Only after

losing everything I owned and finding myself bankrupt did I think
that risk should be factored in,
even mathematically. It took my
waking up in "intensive care" to
realize how dumb and dangerous
this myth is. Life hit me hard
enough to get my attention and
teach me. According to Proverbs
22:7: "The rich rules over the poor,

Myths vs. Truth	
Myth:	Playing the Lotto and other forms of gambling will make you rich
Truth:	Lotto and Power Ball are a tax on the poor and people who can't do math.

and the borrower is servant to the lender" (NKJV). I was confronted with
this Scripture and had to make a conscious decision of who was right—
my broke finance professor, who taught that debt is a tool, or God, who
showed obvious disdain for debt. Beverly Sills had it right when she said,
"There is no shortcut to anyplace worth going."

*What a financial and emotional
mess I was in! I had a master's
degree from the financial arena
and had over $150,000 (yes, that
is four zeros) in debt! I'm one of
those "broke finance professors"
Dave talks about! Hey, I had some
really fun stuff, but I couldn't
enjoy it because of all the debt it caused. I was really paying what
Dave refers to as "stupid tax," doing something stupid that costs
you money!*

*So I decided to make a change. I sold my motor coach and got on
a written budget for the first time in my life. To make a long story
short, I've worked my way out of $116,000 of the debt! I don't*

have as many toys now, but I have a lot of peace. I am actually get-
ting good at my budget, which provides a lot more hope and direc-
tion than my degree and toys did. If you've got an income, you need
The Total Money Makeover. It will be the best thing you've ever
done for yourself, your family, and your money. If I'd had this plan
forty years ago, I have no doubt that I'd be a millionaire today.
DEBT IS NOT A TOOL!

> *Camille Adcock (age 61)*
> *School Counselor*

I have found that if you look into the lives of the kind of people you want to be like, you will find common themes. If you want to be skinny, study skinny people, and if you want to be rich, do what lots of rich people do, not what some mythsayer says to do. The Forbes 400 is a list of the richest 400 people in America as rated by *Forbes* magazine. When surveyed, 75 percent of the Forbes 400 (rich people, not your broke brother-in-law with an opinion) said the best way to build wealth is to become and stay debt-free. Walgreen's, Cisco, Microsoft, and Harley-Davidson are run debt-free. I have met with thousands of millionaires in my years as a financial counselor, and I have never met one who said he made it all with Discover Card bonus points. They all lived on less than they made and spent only when they had cash. No payments.

History also teaches us that debt wasn't always a way of life; in fact, three of the biggest lenders today were founded by people who hated debt. Sears now makes more money on credit than on the sale of merchandise. They are not a store; they are a lender with some stuff out front. However, in 1910 the Sears catalog stated, "Buying on Credit Is Folly." J. C. Penney department stores make millions annually on their plastic, but their founder was nicknamed James "Cash" Penney because he detested the use of debt. Henry Ford thought debt was a lazy man's method to purchase items, and his philosophy was so ingrained in Ford Motor Company that Ford didn't offer financing until ten years after General Motors did. Now, of course, Ford Motor Credit is one of the most profitable of Ford Motor's operations. The old school saw the folly of debt; the new school saw the opportunity to take advantage of the consumer with debt.

You have probably heard a lot of the sub-myths, which fall in line behind the big one that says, "Debt is a tool." So that we leave no stone unturned, let's review and debunk each of the myths spread by a culture that has officially bought the lie.

Myth: **If I loan money to friends or relatives, I am helping them.**

Truth: **If I loan money to a friend or relative, the relationship will be strained or destroyed. The only relationship that would be enhanced is the kind resulting from one party's being the master and the other party a servant.**

The old joke is that if you loan your brother-in-law $100 and he never speaks to you again, was it worth the investment? We have all experienced loaning someone money and finding an immediate distancing in the relationship. Joan called my radio show one day complaining about how a loan had ruined her relationship with one of her best friends at work. She had loaned the lady, a broke single mom, $50 until payday. Payday came and went, and her friend—someone she used to talk to at lunch every day, someone who was her confidante and sounding board—now avoided her. Shame and guilt had entered the scene with no provocation. We don't control how debt affects relationships; debt does that independently of what we want. The borrower is servant to the lender; and you change the spiritual dynamic of relationships when you loan loved ones money. They are no longer friend, uncle, or child; they are now your servant. I know some of you think that is overstated, but tell me why Thanksgiving dinner tastes different when a loan has been served. Eating with your master is different from eating with your family.

Joan was really torn up about losing this friendship. I asked her if the friendship was worth $50. She gushed that it was worth many times that, so I told her to call her friend and tell her the debt was forgiven, a gift.

The borrower is servant to the lender.	The forgiveness of the debt helped her remove the master-servant dynamic from the relationship. Of course, it would be better if that dynamic had never entered the scene. I also suggested two stipu-lations to the forgiveness of the debt: first, that the

friend agree to help someone in need someday; and second, that she never loan friends money. Let's break the myth chain. In Joan's case, the myth chain of loaning a friend money will be broken only if they both learn their lesson. The lesson is that while it is fine to *give* money to friends in need if you have it, loaning them money will mess up relationships.

I have dealt with hundreds of strained and destroyed families where well-meaning people loaned money to "help." Parents loan the twenty-five year old newly married couple the down payment money for the first home. It all seems so noble and nice until the daughter-in-law catches the disapproving glances at the mention of the couple's up-coming vacation. She knows the meaning of the glances, that she should check with these well-meaning, noble parents-in-law before she buys toilet paper until the loan is repaid. A lifetime of resentment can be born right there. The grandfather loans the twenty-year-old $25,000 to purchase that new four-wheel-drive truck he "needs." Of course, the loan is at 6 percent, much better than Junior can get at the bank and much better than Grandpa gets from his CD at the bank. Everyone wins, or do they? What happens when Junior loses his job and can't pay Grandpa, who is from the old school where you dig ditches till midnight if you have to in order to honor your word? Now Junior and Grandpa are at odds, so Junior sells the truck and pays Grandpa the

$19,000 he gets for it. Grandpa hadn't taken a lien on the title, so he now expects broke, angry, and unemployed Junior to repay the balance of $6,000. Grandpa will never see his $6,000 or his grandson again. In some perverted twist of the myth, mixed with shame and guilt, Junior's mind somehow concocts that this is all Grandpa's fault, and he abandons the relationship.

Hundreds of times I've seen relationships strained and sometimes destroyed. We all have, but we continue to believe the myth that a loan to a loved one is a blessing. It isn't; it is a curse. Don't put that burden on any relationship you care about.

Myth: **By co-signing a loan, I am helping a friend or relative.**

Truth: **Be ready to repay the loan; the bank wants a co-signer for a reason, which is that they don't expect the friend or relative to pay.**

Think with me for a moment. If debt is the most aggressively marketed product in our culture today, if lenders must meet sales quotas for "loan production," if lenders can project the likelihood of a loan's going into default with unbelievable accuracy—if all these things are true, and the lending industry has denied your friend or relative a loan, there is little doubt the potential borrower is trouble just looking for a place to happen. Yet people across America make the very unwise (yes, dumb) decision to co-sign for someone else every day.

> We continue to believe the myth that a loan to a loved one is a blessing.

The lender requires a cosigner because there is a very high statistical chance that the applicant won't pay. So why do we appoint ourselves as the generous, all-knowing, benevolent helper to override the judgment of an industry that is foaming at the mouth to lend money, and yet has deemed our friend or relative a deadbeat looking for a place to fail, or at least a loan default looking for a new home? Why do we co-sign knowing full well the inherent problems?

We enter this ridiculous situation only on emotion. Intellect could not take us on this ride. We "know" they will pay because we "know" them. Wrong. Parents co-sign for a young couple to buy a home. Why do they need a cosigner? Because they couldn't afford the home! Parents co-sign for a teenager to buy a car. Why would parents do this? "So he can learn to be responsible." No, what the teenager has learned is, if you can't pay for something, buy it anyway.

The sad thing is that those of us who have co-signed loans know how they end up. We end up paying them, but only after our credit is damaged or ruined. If you co-sign for a car, the lender will not contact you when the loan is paid late every month, but your credit is damaged every month. The lender will not contact you before they repossess the car, but you now have a repo on your credit report. They will contact you to pay the difference between the debt and the below-wholesale repo price they got for the car, which is called a deficit. If the lender did contact you, there is nothing you can legally do to force the sale of the car, because you don't own it; you are merely on the hook for the debt. When you co-sign on a house you will get the same results.

According to Proverbs 17:18, "It's stupid to guarantee someone else's loan" (CEV). That pretty well sums it up. Just like trying to bless a loved one with a loan, many people are trying to help by co-signing, and the result is damaged credit and damaged or destroyed relationships. I have co-signed loans and ended up paying them; one poor guy co-signed for me, and he ended up paying when I went broke. If you truly want to help someone, give money. If you don't have it, then don't sign up to pay it, because you likely will.

I see cases of people caught in the co-signing trap every day on *The Dave Ramsey Show*, our radio talk show. Kevin called to complain that a mortgage company was counting his co-signing for his mom's car against him as a debt even though she had insurance that would pay the loan if she died. Of course they count it, Kevin; it is a debt you are liable for! The mortgage company isn't worrying about her dying; they are worried about her not paying, which would require Kevin to make her car payments and then possibly not be able to pay his mortgage.

Joe, another caller, was surprised to find he was on the hook for $16,000 on a mobile home he co-signed for fifteen years ago. Ten years ago his brother's mobile home was repo'ed, and the bank sold it for $16,000 less than was owed; now, ten years later, the bank caught up with Joe and wanted its money. Joe was angry that this could happen! Most cosigners have no concept of the trip they've signed up for.

That sums up co-signing: broken hearts and broken wallets.

Brian e-mailed me about his girlfriend's car. It seems ol' Brian co-signed for a $5,000 car for his sweetie. Sweetie took off with the car, he can't find her, and, surprise of surprises, she isn't making the payments. Now, either his credit shows him as a deadbeat, or he makes payments on a car he can't find for a girl he doesn't want to find. That sums up co-signing: broken hearts and broken wallets. That's how co-signing usually goes, so unless you are looking for a broken heart and a broken wallet, don't do it.

Myth: **Cash Advance, Payday Loans, Rent-to-Own, Title Pawning, and Tote-the-Note Car Lots are needed to help lower-income people get ahead.**

Truth: **These rip-off examples of predatory lending are designed to take advantage of lower-income people and benefit only the owners of the companies making the loans.**

Lower-income people will remain at the bottom of the socioeconomic ladder if they fall for these rip-offs. These "lenders" (or, as I like to call them, "the scum of the scum") are bottom feeders and legally make themselves rich on the backs of the poor or those soon to be poor. The lending rates of these types of operations are over 100 percent interest, and if you want to stay on the bottom, keep dealing with these guys. You know why these types of operations are located only at the poor end of town? Because rich people won't play. That is how they got to be rich people.

The Payday Loan is one of the fastest-growing trash lenders out there. You write a hot check for $225, dated one week from now, which will be payday. They will give you $200 cash on the spot. All for a mere $25 service charge, which equates to over 650 percent interest annually! Mike called my talk show recently and was caught in a web of Payday Loans. He had not yet had a Total Money Makeover and was still spending like always. He kept adding loan after loan until he couldn't beat the shell game he had created. Basically, Mike had borrowed from one trash lender to pay another, and by doing this again and again had created a cycle of financial death. He was panicked because he was being threatened with criminal charges, for writing bad checks, by the very places that have a business model based on postdated, "bad" checks. This type of business is legalized loan-sharking. The sad thing is that the only way out for Mike is to pop the balloon. He has to stop paying them, close his accounts, and then meet with each lender to work out payment arrangements. That will mean extra jobs and selling things around the house.

The classic Tote-the-Note Car Lot is no better. Most of these transactions involve older, cheaper cars. The dealer purchases these cars and sells them for a down payment equal to what he paid for the car, so the payments at 18 to 38 percent interest paid weekly are all gravy. Tow trucks all over town recognize these exact cars because the car being sold has been sold many times and repeatedly repo'ed by the dealer. Every time the dealer sells the car, his return on investment skyrockets. The payments could have purchased the car for cash in a matter of weeks; in fact, the down payment could have purchased the car if the buyer had been a little more savvy.

Rent-to-Own is one of the worst examples of the little Red-Faced Kid in "I want it now!" mode. The Federal Trade Commission continues to investigate this industry because the effective interest rates in rent-to-own transactions are over 1,800 percent on average. People rent items they can't possibly afford to buy because they look only at "how much a week" and think, *I can afford this.* Well, when you look at the numbers, no one can afford this. The average washer and dryer will cost you just $20 per week for 90 weeks. That is a total of $1,800 for a washer and dryer you could have bought new at full retail price for $500 and slightly used for $200. As my old professor used to say about the "own" part of Rent-to-Own, "You should *live* so long!"

> We buy things we don't need with money we don't have in order to impress people we don't like.

If you had saved $20 per week for just 10 weeks, you could have bought the scratch-and-dent model off the floor at the same Rent-to-Own store for $200! Or you could have bought a used set out of the classifieds. It pays to look past the weekend and suffer through going to the Laundromat with your quarters. When you think short-term, you always set yourself up for being ripped off by a predatory lender. If the Red-Faced Kid ("I want it, and I want it now!") rules your life, you will stay broke!

If you use Payday Loans, Tote-the-Note, and Rent-to-Own, please understand that you are being destroyed financially. These businesses feed on the working poor, and you must avoid them at all costs if you want to win with money.

Myth: "Ninety days same as cash" equals using other people's money for free.

Truth: Ninety days is not the same as cash.

The silly marketing that America falls for has resulted in this: We buy things we don't need with money we don't have in order to impress people we don't like. "Ninety days same as cash" has exploded in furniture, electronics, and appliance sales. I recently met a lady who financed her dog at the pet store. "But I paid him off early," she said proudly. Good thing for Rover that he was able to avoid the repo man.

Ninety days is NOT the same as cash for three basic reasons: One, if you will flash cash ($100 bills) in front of a manager who has a sales quota to meet, you will likely get a discount. If you can't get a discount, go to the competitor and get one. You do not get the discount when you sign up for the finance plan.

Dave Rants ...

Whole Life insurance is a horrible product. Why would you pay someone interest on your own savings? That's backward, and it does not make you smart.

Two, most people don't pay off the debt in the allotted time. Nationally, 88 percent of these contracts convert to debt—a debt where you are charged a rip-off interest rate of 24 to 38 percent, and they back-charge you to the date of purchase. Please don't tell me you are the one who is actually going to pay it off. A $1,000 stereo (don't forget, you didn't get a discount) will not make you rich in ninety days. But $1,000 left in a savings account at 3 percent annual interest will earn you $7.50 in ninety days. Wow, some financial genius you are!

Three, you are playing with snakes, and you will get bitten. Marge called my radio show with this little story. She and her husband purchased a big-screen TV at a nationally known electronics store. This couple paid off the big screen slightly early to be sure they would not be tricked into the interest being back-charged. No such luck. They had declined the disability and life insurance (for a charge of $174), but apparently the salesperson had fraudulently initialed the contract in that area, something that happens more frequently than you think. So although our brilliant couple thought they had paid off the TV, they still had a balance and were charged with the interest back through the entire deal. They were fighting it, but it would take hiring a handwriting expert and going to court with an attorney to avoid paying a bill under $1,000, even though they did not owe it. That is disheartening. The little game of "we are going to use your money for free" backfired big-time. I recently purchased a TV with a built-in DVD player in that exact same store for cash; I got a discount and walked out with my TV. No hassle, no court costs, no interest, no lies.

No, Virginia, ninety days is NOT the same as cash.

Myth: **Car payments are a way of life; you'll always have one.**

Truth: **Staying away from car payments by driving reliable used cars is what the average millionaire does; that is how he or she became a millionaire.**

Taking on a car payment is one of the dumbest things people do to destroy their chances of building wealth. The car payment is most folks' largest payment except for their home mortgage, so it steals more money from the income than virtually anything else. *USA Today* notes that the average car payment is $378 over 55 months. Most people get a car payment and keep it throughout their lives. As soon as a car is paid off, they get another payment because they "need" a new car. If you keep a $378 car payment throughout your life, which is "normal," you miss the opportunity to save that money. If you invested $378 per month from age 25 to age 65, a normal working lifetime, in the average mutual fund averaging 12 percent (the 70-year stock market average), you would have $4,447,084.01 at age 65. Hope you like the car!

Some of you had your nose in the air as intellectual snobs when I illustrated how bad Rent-to-Own is because you would never enter such an establishment, and yet you are doing worse on your car deal. If you put

$378 per month in a cookie jar for just ten months, you have almost $4,000 for a cash car. I am not suggesting you drive a $4,000 car your whole life, but that is how you start without debt. Then you can save the same amount again and trade up to an $8,000 car ten months later and up to a $12,000 car ten months after that. In just thirty months, or two and one-half years, you can drive a paid-for $12,000 car, never having made a payment, and never have to make payments again. Taking on car payments because everyone else does it does not make it smart. Will your broke relatives and friends make fun of your junk car while you do this? Sure they will, but that is a very good sign you are on the right track.

Having been a millionaire and gone broke, I dug my way out by making a decision about looking good versus being good. Looking good is when your broke friends are impressed by what you drive,

> ## SHOCKING STATS
>
> Over 97% of people don't systematically pay extra on their mortgage.

and being good is having more money than they have.

Are you starting to realize that The Total Money Makeover is also in your heart? You have to reach the point that what people think is not your primary motivator. Reaching the goal is the motivator. Do you remember the circus game where you swing the large hammer over your head to hit the lever to send a weight up a pole to ring the bell? You reach the point that you want to ring the bell! Who cares if you are a ninety-eight-pound weakling with gawky form? The girls are still impressed when the bell is rung. When the goal, not how you look, begins to matter, you are on your way to a Total Money Makeover.

Today I drive very nice, very expensive, slightly used cars, but it wasn't always that way. After going broke, I drove a borrowed 400,000-mile Cadillac with a vinyl roof torn loose so that it filled up with air like a parachute. The predominant color on this car was Bondo. I drove the

Bondo buggy for what felt like ten years during one three-month period. I had dropped from a Jaguar to a borrowed Bondo buggy! This was not fun, but I knew that if I would live like no one else, later I could live like no one else. Today I am convinced that my wife and I are able to do anything we want financially partially because of the car sacrifices we made in the early days. I believe, with everything within me, that we are winning because of the heart change that allowed us to drive old, beat-up cars in order to win. If you insist on driving new cars with payments your whole life, you will literally blow a life's fortune on them. If you are willing to sacrifice for a while, you can have your life's fortune *and* drive quality cars. I'd opt for the millionaire's strategy.

Myth: **Leasing a car is what sophisticated people do. You should lease things that go down in value and take the tax advantage.**

Truth: **Consumer advocates, noted experts, and a good calculator will confirm that the car lease is the most expensive way to operate a vehicle.**

Consumer Reports, Smart Money magazine, and my calculator tell me that leasing a car is the worst possible way to acquire a vehicle. In effect, you are renting to own. The cost of capital, which is the interest rate, is extremely high, yet most new car deals this year will be a fleece . . . I mean, a lease. They're *baaaadd!* Sorry, that's my impression of a sheep getting "fleeced." The auto industry lobbyists are so powerful that the law does not require full lender disclosure. The industry argues that you are merely renting, which you are, so they shouldn't be required to show you the actual effective interest rate. The Federal Trade Commission requires a truth-in-lending statement when you buy a

> Most new car deals this year will be a fleece . . . I mean, a lease.

car or get a mortgage, but not on a lease, so you don't know what you are paying unless you are very good with a calculator. Having seen several hundred lease agreements entered into by people I have counseled, my financial calculator confirms that the average interest rate is 14 percent.

Shouldn't you lease or rent things that go down in value? Not necessarily, and the math doesn't work on a car for sure. Follow me through this example: If you rent (lease) a car with a value of $22,000 for three years, and when you turn it in at the end of that three-year lease the car is worth $10,000, someone has to cover the $12,000 loss. You're not stupid, so you know that General Motors, Ford, Chrysler, or any of the other auto giants aren't going to put together a plan to lose money. Your fleece/lease payment is designed to cover the loss in value ($12,000 spread over 36 months is equal to $333 per month), plus provide profit (the interest you pay).

Where did you get a deal in that? You didn't! On top of that, there is the charge of 10 to 17 cents per mile for going over the allotted miles and the penalties everyone turning in a lease has experienced for "excessive wear and tear," which takes into account every little nick, dent, carpet tear, smudge, or smell. You end up writing a large check just to walk away after renting your car. The whole idea of the back-end penalties is twofold: to get you to fleece/lease another one so you can painlessly roll the gotchas into the new lease, and to make sure the car company makes money.

Smart Money magazine quotes the National Auto Dealers Association (NADA) as stating the average new car purchased for cash makes the dealer an $82 profit. When the dealer can get you to finance with them, they sell the financing contract and make an average of $775 per car! But if they can get you to fleece the car, the dealer can sell that fleece to the local bank or GMAC, Ford Motor Credit, Chrysler Credit, Toyota Credit, etc., for an average of $1,300! The typical car dealer makes their money in the finance office and the shop, not in the sale of new cars.

Car fleecing is exploding because dealers know it is their largest profit center. We live in a culture that quit asking, "How much?" and instead asks, "How much down, and how much a month?" If you look at only the monthly outlay, then you will always fleece, because it almost always costs less down and less a month, but in the long run, it is much more expensive. Once again, the Red-Faced Kid bought something he couldn't afford using an unwise method and then attempted to justify his stupidity. That red-faced stuff won't work if you want a Total Money Makeover.

Craig called my radio show to argue about leasing because his CPA said he should lease a car. (Proof that some CPAs can't add, or at least don't take the time to!) Craig owned his own business and thought the tax write-off if his business owned the car made fleecing smart. Craig had the $20,000 cash to buy a one-year-old car just like the one he wanted, but instead he was going to fleece a new $30,000 one. He missed two important points. First, 98 percent of fleecing is done on a new car, which rapidly loses value, not a wise business decision. Second, creating an unneeded business expense for the sake of a tax write-off is bad math.

Let's say that Craig fleeced a car for $416 per month, $5,000 per year, and used it 100 percent for business (which is highly unlikely and most times won't survive an audit). If you have a tax write-off of $5,000, you don't pay taxes on that money. If Craig didn't have the $5,000 write-off, he would pay taxes on that $5,000, which would be about $1,500 in taxes. So Craig's CPA's suggestion that he send the car company $5,000 to keep from sending the government $1,500 sounds as though he can't add. Plus, Craig now is responsible for a $30,000 car that is dropping in value instead of a $20,000 car that took the worst drop in value during its first year.

My company owns my cars, which we purchased used. We are able to straight-line depreciate those cars or write off the mileage. If you drive inexpensive cars in your business and put high mileage on them, take the mileage deduction. If you, like me, drive expensive cars but do not put many miles on them, take the straight-line depreciation. Both tax deductions are available to you without having a stupid car payment. If you don't own a business and didn't understand everything I just said about tax write-offs, etc., don't worry. Just know that, as a wise business owner, you don't want to fleece a car.

Myth: **You can get a good deal on a new car at 0 percent interest.**

Truth: **A new car loses 60 percent of its value in the first four years; that isn't 0 percent.**

We have discussed the new-car purchase in its various forms for the last several pages. No, you can't afford a new car unless you are a millionaire

> The average millionaire drives a two-year-old car with no payments.

and can therefore afford to lose thousands of dollars, all in the name of the neat new car smell. A good used car that is less than three years old is as reliable or more reliable than a new car. A new $28,000 car will lose about $17,000 of value in the first four years you own it. That is almost $100 per week in lost value. To understand what I'm talking about, open your window on your way to work once a week and throw out a $100 bill.

The average millionaire drives a two-year-old car with no payments. He or she simply bought it. The average millionaire is unwilling to take the loss that a new car dishes out; that is how they became millionaires. I am not saying you will never drive a brand-new car, but until you have so much money you can lose big bucks and not notice, you can't afford the luxury. The car dealer will tell you that you are "buying someone else's problems." Then why do they sell used cars? Wouldn't that be morally wrong? The truth is that most slightly used cars have gotten all the kinks worked out of them and were not traded because they were bad cars.

Since almost 80 percent of the new cars this year will be fleeced, more than likely you are buying a car that came off a lease. My last two car purchases were one- and two-year lease turn-ins with low miles.

If you understand what I am saying about this huge loss in value, you now realize that 0 percent interest isn't really "no cost." While the money to borrow isn't technically costing you, you are losing so much in value that you have still been taken. Zero percent, however, is used quite often by guys (seldom gals) to rationalize their "need" for some new wheels. So even though the interest rate is attractive, pass it up because the whole transaction still means throwing $100 bills out the window each week.

Some people want to buy a new car for the warranty. If you lose $17,000 of value over four years, on average you have paid too much for a warranty. You could have completely rebuilt the car twice for $17,000! Also, keep in mind that most manufacturers' warranties will still cover you when buying a slightly used car. (We will address buying an extended warranty on a used car in the next chapter.) Of course, when you begin your Total Money Makeover, you may have an old beater, but the goal is to avoid the temptation of the 0 percent interest myth and get into quality used cars.

Myth: **You should get a credit card to build your credit.**

Truth: **You won't use credit with your Total Money Makeover, except maybe for a mortgage, and you don't need a credit card for that.**

The best myth is the "build your credit" myth. Bankers, car dealers, and unknowledgeable mortgage lenders have told America for years to "build your credit." This myth means we have to get debt so we can get more debt because debt is how we get stuff. Those of us who have had a Total Money Makeover have found that cash buys stuff better than debt.

But if I were selling debt, as the banker is, I also would tell you to get debt to get more debt. This is, however, a myth.

Yes, you will need to "build your credit" by borrowing and repaying debt in a timely fashion if you want to live a life of credit cards, student loans, and car payments. Not me. The one question we must answer is, "How do I get a home mortgage?" Later, I will introduce you to the 100 percent down plan, or if you must, how to settle for a fifteen-year fixed-rate mortgage. But if you want that fifteen-year fixed rate with a payment that is no more than 25 percent of your take-home pay so I won't yell about it, don't you need credit? No.

> You can get a mortgage if you have lived right.

You will need to find a mortgage company that does actual underwriting. That means they are professional enough to process the details of your life instead of using only a Beacon score (lending for dummies). You can get a mortgage if you have lived right. Let me define "lived right."

You can qualify for a Conventional fifteen-year fixed-rate loan if:

- You have paid your landlord early or on time for two years.
- You have been in the same career field for two years.
- You have a good down payment, which is more than "nothing down."
- You have no other credit, good or bad.
- You are not trying to take too big a loan. A payment that totals 25 percent of take-home is conservative and will help you qualify.

Don't let anyone tell you to go into debt to make way for a mortgage; that is a lie. A quality mortgage professional can get you into a home if he or she knows how to do underwriting. As for building credit for the other stuff, leave that to the losers. With your Total Money Makeover, you won't be taking on that kind of debt anyway.

Myth: **You need a credit card to rent a car, check into a hotel, or buy on-line.**

Truth: **A debit card will do all that.**

The Visa debit card or other check cards that are connected to your checking account give you the ability to do virtually anything a credit card will do. I carry a debit card on my personal account and one on my business and do not have one credit card. Of course, you must have money before you can buy something with a debit card, but paying for things with money you have now is part of your Total Money Makeover. Some rental-car places don't take debit cards, but most do. I don't do business with Hertz or Avis because they don't take debit cards, and they are too high anyway. Most of the others will take the debit card, but you need to check in advance. I buy things on-line and stay in hotels using my debit card all the time. In fact, I travel all over the nation several times a year speaking and doing appearances, and my debit card allows me access to the best things life has to offer with no debt.

Remember, there is one thing the debit card *won't* do: get you into debt.

Myth: **The debit card has more risk than a credit card.**

Truth: **Nope.**

Some of you were concerned when I mentioned buying things on-line and reserving hotels with a debit card. The perception is that it's riskier to conduct that kind of business with a debit card. Supposed financial experts have spread this myth to the point that it is virtually urban legend. The fact is, Visa's regulations require the member bank to afford the debit card the exact same protections in cases of theft or fraud. If you have any doubt, read this quote from Visa's own Web site:

Visa's Zero Liability policy means 100% protection for you. Visa's enhanced policy guarantees maximum protection against fraud. You now have complete liability protection for all of your card transactions that take place on the Visa system. Should someone steal your card number while you're shopping, online or off, you pay nothing for their fraudulent activity. If you notice fraudulent activity on your card, promptly contact your financial institution to report it. It is important to continually monitor your monthly statement to identify any unauthorized transactions.

Visa's Zero Liability policy took effect April 4, 2000, and is a great improvement on the previous policy. The former policy required that you report fraudulent activity within two business days of discovery. After this two-day period, you could be held responsible for up to $50 of the unauthorized charges. With the new Zero Liability policy, you're no longer required to report fraudulent activity within two days and you're not responsible for any fraudulent transactions made over the Visa network. The Zero Liability policy covers all Visa credit and debit card transactions processed over the Visa network—on-line or off.

Myth: **If you pay off your credit card every month, you get the free use of someone else's money.**

Truth: **CardTrak says 60 percent don't pay off their credit cards every month.**

As I said, when you play with snakes, you get bitten. I have heard all the bait put out there to lure the unsuspecting into the pit. A free hat, airline miles, brownie points back, free use of someone else's money, a discount at the register—the list goes on to get you to sign up for a credit card. Have you ever asked why they work so hard to get you involved? The answer is that you lose and they win.

You won't wear the hat, and *Consumer Reports* says 75 percent of the airline miles are never redeemed. Next time you are in the store that gave you a discount for signing up for a card, you will have forgotten your cash, you'll use the card, and the cycle begins. Maybe you think, *I pay mine off, so I'm using their money. I'm winning.* Wrong again. A study by Dunn and Bradstreet showed that the credit-card user spends 12 to 18 percent more when using credit instead of cash. It hurts when you spend cash, and, therefore, you spend less.

> When you play with snakes, you get bitten.

The big question is, What do millionaires do? They don't get rich with free hats, brownie points, air miles, and use of someone else's money. What do broke people do? They use credit cards. An American Bankruptcy Institute study of bankruptcy filers reveals that 69 percent of filers say credit-card debt caused the bankruptcy. Broke people use credit cards; rich people don't. I rest my case.

M*y huge debt problems were mostly due to my mishandling of credit cards.*

After I got my first job and had worked for about six months, I decided to take a small vacation. I went to the bank to see if I could borrow a small amount of money. The nice people at the bank said they couldn't loan me any money, but they told me I could get a free credit card. This was my introduction to credit cards.

Of course, my credit limit on the card was for more money than I needed, but before long I found that I had spent the maximum. Not to worry though, the company sent me a note telling me that because I was such a good customer, they were going to increase my limit, which meant more instant cash for me. In addition, they told me that because I was such a good customer, I didn't have to make a payment during the holiday season that year. What they did not tell me was that the interest, at 22 percent, would continue to grow!

I thought it was prestigious to have as many credit cards as I could get. The number of cards I was able to acquire appeared limitless. I had Gold cards, Platinum cards, and cards through all kinds of major companies, plus specific stores and catalogs.

Then, just as the debt got to be a real challenge to pay, along came the introductory-low-interest cards. They promised a very low interest rate for the first few months. As long as you didn't read the small print, it looked like a real deal! So I applied and received several of those cards as well.

By this time, my credit-card debt alone was well into the $30,000 range. I had reached the point where I had to use credit cards to purchase food, to pay rent, and even to bounce money from one card to another to make the monthly payments. I calculated that if I could simply pay the minimum on each card and not purchase anything new, I could pay them all off—in about twenty-two years!

I now follow the teaching of The Total Money Makeover and encourage people to STAY AWAY from credit cards!

Anonymous

Myth: **Make sure your teenager gets a credit card so he or she will learn to be responsible with money.**

Truth: **Getting a credit card for your teenager is an excellent way to teach him or her to be financially irresponsible. That's why teens are now the number-one target of credit-card companies.**

The past several pages have been devoted to the evils of credit cards, so I'm not going to repeat myself in the case of teenagers. I'll only add that throwing your teen into a pool of sharks is a sure way to guarantee a lifetime of heartache for them and for you. I will also tell you that over 80 percent of graduating college seniors have credit-card debt before they even have a job! The credit-card marketers have done such a thorough job that a credit card is seen as a rite of passage into adulthood. American teens view themselves as adults if they have a credit card, a cell phone, and a driver's license. Sadly, none of these "accomplishments" are in any way associated with real adulthood.

> **You are not teaching your sixteen-year-old child to spend responsibly when you give him a credit card.**

You are not teaching your sixteen-year-old child to spend responsibly when you give him a credit card any more than you are teaching gun responsibility by letting him sleep with a loaded automatic weapon with the safety off. In both cases, you as a parent are being stupid. People with common sense don't give sixteen-year-olds beer to teach them how to hold their liquor. By giving a teenager a credit card, the parent, the one with supposed credibility, introduces a financially harmful substance and endorses its use, which is dumb but unfortunately very normal in today's families. Parents must instead teach the teenager to just say no. Anyone visiting a college campus in recent years has been shocked at the aggressive and senseless marketing of credit cards to people who don't have jobs. The results can be devastating. Recently, two college students in Oklahoma gave up on their credit-card debt and committed suicide with the bills lying on the bed beside them.

I was never told how to manage my money, never taught that there were consequences to overspending. When I went off to college, I was quick to sign up for the university's credit card. I was intrigued that 10 percent of everything I spent went back to the school, and,

hey, I wanted to be a big supporter! (10 percent of $200 is 20 big bucks!) Besides, I knew I would only use it for emergencies. Yeah, right!

Well, I remember the day I got the card. I was in my dorm, bored out of my mind, flipping through my mail, and there it was, with a picture of the school on it and everything! I was only going to use it for "emergencies," after I used it one time in order to activate it.

I went to the mall and activated it, all right—all $200 of it—on a cheap suit with a matching belt. I'll never forget it. I maxed out my card the first day I had it! Visa gladly raised my limit and would continue doing so, several times over the next four years. I walked out of college with a bachelor of science degree and over $13,000 in credit-card debt!

I really wasn't that concerned about it, because as long as I made the minimum payment I was fine—yeah, right! Well, all I can tell you is that I couldn't get ahead. I felt trapped, and it was just too easy to use the credit cards.

Today, I'm totally debt-free, but it wasn't without a lot of pain. Debt kept me from achieving. There was so much my wife and I couldn't afford; so much of our peace was being robbed.

We learned our lessons, however, thanks to The Total Money Makeover plan.

> *Bill Hampton (age 32)*
> *Vice President,*
> *The Lampo Group, Inc.*

Vince called my radio show with a problem that has become a trend. Vince signed up for multiple cards during his sophomore year at college to get the free campus T-shirt. He wasn't going to use the cards unless there was an emergency, but there was an "emergency" every week, and soon he was $15,000 in debt. He couldn't make the payments, so he quit school to get a job. The problem was, without his degree his earnings were minimal. Worse than that, he also had $27,000 in student loans. Student loans aren't payable while you are in school, but when you leave school by graduating or quitting, the payments begin. Vince was one scared twenty-one-year-old with $42,000 in debt, but making only $15,000 per year. What's scary is that Vince is "normal." The American Bankruptcy Institute reveals that 19 percent of the people who filed for bankruptcy last year were college students. That means one in five bankruptcy filings were by very young people who started their lives as financial failures. Do you still think it is wise to give a teen a card? I hope not.

The reason why lenders market so aggressively to teens is brand loyalty. The lenders' studies have found that we consumers are very loyal to the first bank that certifies our adulthood by issuing us plastic. When I am doing an appearance and cutting up credit cards, the emotional attachment many people have to the first card they got in college is amazing. They clutch it like it is an old friend. Brand loyalty is real.

Several hundred schools across America are using our high school curriculum called "Financial Peace, for the Next Generation." The results have been staggering. Teens latch onto The Total Money Makeover before they need one. A recent graduate of the program, fifteen-year-old Chelsea, said, "I think this class has totally changed my life. Whenever I see someone using a credit card, I think, *Whoa! How could they do that to their life?* I always thought you had to have credit-card payments, house payments, and car payments. Now, I realize you don't have to." Very cool, Chelsea.

Kid-Branding

You have to start teaching kids early because "kid-branding" is now commonplace. I see kid-branding when I look at the back of a box of Raisin Bran and see "Visa . . . the official card of Whoville . . . from *How the Grinch Stole Christmas*." I am not the target of this ad; my eleven-year-old is. Lenders are teaching kids earlier and earlier their message of reliance on plastic. A few years back, Mattel put out "Cool Shopping

Barbie," which was sponsored by MasterCard. Of course this "cool" babe had her own MasterCard. When she scanned her card, the cash register said, "Credit approved." There was so much consumer backlash that Mattel pulled the product. This year, Barbie came out with the "Barbie Cash Register," and apparently this lady does a lot of shopping. The register comes with its own American Express card. Why are these companies selling to our small children? Kid-branding intends to influence card choices later in life. This is immoral.

Again, we decided to combat kid-branding with our own antidote. Financial Peace Jr. is a collection of aids to help parents teach their children (ages three to twelve) about money. Of course, you can teach the principles without the kit, but, either way, they need to learn them. In my home, we used the same techniques to teach our kids four things to do with money. We wanted to create teachable moments so that the kid-branding would be counteracted by common sense. We teach our kids to work—not like being at some boot camp, but that doing chores equals money. Our kids are on commission, not allowance. Work and get paid; don't work and don't get paid. It's just like the real world. Our children put their newly earned money in envelopes labeled Save, Spend, and Give. When a child learns to work, save, spend, and give under a mature parent's direction, the child can avoid the messages that say a credit card equals prosperity.

Myth: **Debt consolidation saves interest, and you have one smaller payment.**

Truth: **Debt consolidation is dangerous because you treat only the symptom.**

Debt CONsolidation—it's nothing more than a con because you think you've done something about the debt problem. The debt is still there, as are the habits that caused it; you just moved it! You can't borrow your way out of debt. You can't get out of a hole by digging out the bottom.

Larry Burkett says debt is not the problem; it is the symptom. I feel debt is the symptom of overspending and undersaving.

A friend of mine works for a debt-consolidation firm whose internal statistics estimate that 78 percent of the time, after someone consolidates his credit-card debt, the debt grows back. Why? He still doesn't have a game plan to either pay cash or not buy at all, and hasn't saved for "unexpected events," which will also become debt.

> Work and get paid; don't work and don't get paid.

Debt consolidation seems appealing because there is a lower interest rate on some of the debt and a lower payment. In almost every case we review though, we find that the lower payment exists not because the rate is actually lower but because the term is extended. If you stay in debt longer, you get a lower payment. If you stay in debt longer, you pay the lender more, which is why they are in the business of debt consolidation. The answer is not the interest rate; the answer is a Total Money Makeover.

Myth: **Borrowing 125 percent on my home is wise because I'll restructure my debt.**

Truth: **You are stuck in the house, which is really dumb.**

On today's radio show I took a call from a desperate man facing bankruptcy. He had borrowed $42,000 on a second mortgage, a rip-off 125 percent loan. Dan's existing balance on his first mortgage was $110,000, making his total new mortgage debt $152,000. Dan's home was worth $125,000, so he owed $27,000 more on his home than it was worth. He lost his job two months ago and luckily has just found a job in another state, but he can't sell his home. He had the same job for sixteen years and thought he had security, but now, just a few months later, he is "in the soup."

My suggestion to Dan was that he call the second mortgage rip-off lender and get an acknowledgment of the truth, that there really isn't any collateral for the loan. They wouldn't foreclose in a hundred years, but they will sue him when the first mortgage company forecloses. So, after asking the second lender to release the lien for whatever proceeds above the first mortgage come from a sale, Dan will sign a note and make payments on the rest. Dan will have payments for years to come on a second mortgage for a home he no longer owns, but like most folks, his second mortgage was to pay off (move) debt he already had on credit cards, medical bills, and other life issues. Today, with a job in another state, Dan would rather have all his old debt back and his home where he could sell it easily.

Myth: If no one used debt, our economy would collapse.

Truth: Nope, it would prosper.

The occasional economics teacher feels the need to pose this ridiculous scenario. My dream is to get as many Americans as possible out of debt with a Total Money Makeover. Unfortunately, I could sell ten million books, and there would still be five billion credit-card offers per year, so there is no danger of my working myself out of a job. The best weight-loss program in the world can never ensure there will be no fat Americans; after all, there are too many McDonald's.

However, let's pretend for the fun of it. What if every single American stopped using debt of any kind in one year? The economy would collapse. What if every single American stopped using debt of any kind over the next fifty years, a gradual TOTAL Money Makeover? The economy would prosper, although banks and other lenders would suffer. Do I see tears anywhere? What would people do if they didn't have any payments? They would save and they would spend, not support banks. Spending by debt-free people would support and prosper the economy.

The economy would be much more stable without the tidal waves caused by "consumer confidence" or the lack thereof. (Consumer confidence is that thing economists use to measure how much you will overspend due to your being giddy about how great the economy is, never taking into consideration that you are going deeply into debt. If the consumer were out of debt and living within his means, the confidence he would have would be well founded.) Saving and investing would cause wealth to be built at an unprecedented level, which would create more stability and spending. Giving would increase, and many social problems would be privatized; thus, the government could get out of the welfare business. Then taxes could come down, and we would have even more wealth. As that great philosopher Austin Powers said, "Capitalism, yeah, baby!" Ahhhh, capitalism is cool. Those who are worried about polarization, the widening gap between the haves and the have-nots, need not look to government to solve the problem; just call for a national Total Money Makeover.

> What would people do if they didn't have any payments?

Debt Is *Not* a Tool

> Debt is not a tool; it is a method to make banks wealthy, not you.

Are you beginning to understand that debt is NOT a tool? This myth and all its little sub-myths have been spread far and wide. Always keep in mind the idea that if you tell a lie often enough, loud enough, and long enough, the myth becomes accepted as a fact. Repetition, volume, and longevity will twist and turn a myth, a lie, into a commonly accepted way of doing things. No more. Debt is not a tool; it is a method to make banks wealthy, not you. The borrower truly is servant to the lender.

Your largest wealth-building asset is your income. When you tie up your income, you lose. When you invest your income, you become wealthy and can do anything you want.

How much could you give every month, save every month, and spend every month if you had no payments? Your income is your greatest wealth-building tool, not debt. Your Total Money Makeover begins with a permanently changed view of the Debt Myths.

4

Money Myths:
The (Non)Secrets of the Rich

Most Money Myths have to do with a lie about a shortcut or a lie about safety. We yearn to become healthy, wealthy, and wise with no effort and with no risk, but it will never happen. Why else is the lottery so successful in pulling in millions of dollars? Why do people stay in jobs they hate, seeking false security? The Total Money Makeover mentality is to live like no one else so later we can live like no one else. A price has to be paid, and there are no shortcuts. While no one goes looking for needless pain, risk, or sacrifice, when something sounds too good to be true, it is. The myths in this chapter are rooted in two basic problems. First is risk denial, thinking total safety is possible and likely. Second is easy wealth, or looking for the magic key to open the treasure chest.

Risk Denial

Risk denial takes several forms in the world of money. Sometimes risk denial is a kind of laziness, when we don't want to take the energy to realize that energy is needed to win. Other times, risk denial is a kind of surrender in which we settle for a bad solution because we are so beat down or beat up that we wave the white flag and do something stupid. At still other times, risk denial can have an active component when we search for a false security that simply doesn't exist. This is the risk denial of someone who keeps a job he or she hates for fourteen years because the company is "secure," only to find life turned upside down by a layoff when the "secure" company files for bankruptcy. Money denial always involves an illusion, followed by disillusionment.

Quick, Easy Money

The second underlying problem is the quest for easy wealth. Quick, easy money is one of the oldest lies, or myths, in the book of the human race. A shortcut, a microwave dinner, instant coffee, and dotcom instant millionaires are things we wish would give us high quality, but they never do. The secrets of the rich don't exist, because the principles aren't a secret. There is no magic key, and if you are looking for one, you've set yourself up for pain and the loss of money. One of my pastors says that living right is not complicated; it may be difficult, but it is not complicated. Living right financially is the same way—it is not complicated; it may be difficult, but it is not complicated.

> The secrets of the rich don't exist, because the principles aren't a secret.

Myth vs. Truth

In addition to Debt Myths, we must dispel several other Money Myths as part of your Total Money Makeover. Most of these Money Myths are rooted in the problems we have already discussed: denial and/or a shortcut mentality.

Myth: **Everything will be fine when I retire. I know I'm not saving yet, but it will be okay.**

Truth: **Ed McMahon isn't coming.**

How can I put this delicately? There is no shining knight headed your way on a white horse to save the day. Wake up! This is the real world where sad old people eat Alpo! Please don't be under the illusion that this government, one that is so inept and dim-witted with money, is going to take great care of you in your golden years. That is your job! This is an emergency! The house is on fire! You have to save. You have to invest in your future. You won't be FINE! Do you get the picture?

We live in the land of plenty, and that has lulled a large percentage of Americans to sleep, thinking everything will be "okay." Things won't be okay unless you make them that way. Your destiny and your dignity are up to you. You are in charge of your retirement. We'll talk about how to take charge of it later in the book, but for now, you'd better be 100 percent convinced that this area deserves your full attention *right now*— not tomorrow or pretty soon. Personally, I don't want to work at McDonald's when I retire—unless it's the one I own on St. Thomas in the U.S. Virgin Islands.

Myth: **Gold is a good investment and will cover me if the economy collapses.**

Truth: **Gold has a poor track record and isn't used when an economy collapses.**

Gold has been sold as a stable investment that everyone should own. Conventional wisdom intones, "Since the beginning of time, gold has been the standard that man has used to exchange goods and services." After making that pitch, the mythsayer will follow up with the statement that in a failed economy, gold is the only thing that will retain its value. "You will have what everyone wants" is how the pitch continues. After hearing these pitches, people buy gold as an investment under the illusion of false security, or risk denial.

The truth is that gold is a lousy investment with a long track record of mediocrity. The average rates of return tracked as far back as Napoleon are around 2 percent gain per year. In recent history, gold has a fifty-year track record of around 4.4 percent, about the same as inflation and just above savings accounts. During that same time frame, you would have made around 12 percent in a good growth-stock mutual fund. During those fifty years though, there has been incredible volatility and tons of risk.

> Gold is a lousy investment with a long track record of mediocrity.

It is important to remember that gold is not used when economies fail. History shows that when an economy completely collapses, the first thing that appears is a black-market barter system, in which people trade items for other items or services. In a primitive culture, items of utility often become the medium of exchange, and the same is temporarily true in a failed economy. A skill, a pair of blue jeans, or a tank of gas becomes very valuable, but not gold coins or nuggets. Usually a new government rises from the ashes, and new paper money or coinage is established. Gold will, at best, play a minor role, and the gold investor will be left with the sick feeling that real estate, canned soup, or knowledge would have been a better hedge against a failed economy.

Myth: **I can get rich quickly and easily if I join these groups, buy this tape set, and work three hours a week.**

Truth: **No one develops and makes a six-figure income on three hours a week.**

I received an e-mail this week from a gentleman offering me a 500-to-1 return on my money. He stated that he has become so enthused about the prospects of this "investment" that he has gotten several of his friends in the deal with him. (Oh no.) He didn't have a lot of time in his busy schedule, but he would make time if I would meet with him. No thanks. I don't know what this is, but I know it is a scam. I am not cynical, but I do know investments. Odds of 500 to 1 don't come through, and I won't waste my time discussing them or trying to find the flaw in the logic. It is a scam, period. Run as fast as you can to get away from these people!

> ### Dum Math & Stupid Tax
>
> **The Answer, My Friend, Is Blowing out the Window**
>
> A new $28,000 car will lose about $17,000 of value in the first four years you own it. To get the same result, you could toss a $100 bill out the window once a week during your commute.

As a younger man I often fell prey to this type of garbage. Later, I used to have meetings with these guys to try to find the flaw. Now I just shake my head—because I know he is heading for pain and loss, and so are his friends.

Have you seen the midnight infomercial about ordering the tape set with the "secrets" so that "you, too," can become wildly wealthy by buying nothing-down real estate or by learning the hidden formula to success in the stock market? Small-business ideas abound, such as getting rich at home by stuffing envelopes and doing medical billings. Be realistic. Envelopes are stuffed by machines at a rate of thousands a minute and at a cost of tenths of a penny; they are not stuffed by a stay-at-home mom trying to supplement the family income! One person in every thousand who attempt the oversold, overdone medical-billing concept does so at a profit. The legitimate, profitable medical biller is usually someone who came from the medical industry, not someone who got ripped off taking a weekend course. Don't fall for this!

Real estate can be purchased for nothing down, but then you owe so much on it that there is no cash flow. You have to "feed" it every month. I bought foreclosure and bankruptcy real estate for years and know it can be done, but the players with cash are the ones who win. The good deals are one in two hundred *if* you are experienced and very good at the business; I worked sixty hours a week, and it took me years to get to a six-figure income in real estate.

The stock market attracts the brightest business minds on the planet. These meganerds study, track, chart, eat, and breathe the stock market and have for generations. Still, every other year a book, or con artist, comes out claiming to have "discovered" little-known keys, patterns, or trends that will "make you rich." The Beardstown Ladies published a *New York Times* best-seller about their cute little quilting group who started investing and discovered how to get unbelievable returns. As it turns out, the whole thing was a fraud; they never got those reported returns, and the publisher got sued. Another book was published on the *Dogs of the Dow*, showing a little-known pattern about buying the worst stocks on the Dow Jones Industrial Average to gain wealth. As it turns out, the author wrote another book about how to invest in bonds, after he had discovered his formula didn't work.

It is really hard to sell books and tapes that teach the necessity of lots of hard work, living on less than you make, getting out of debt, and living on a plan, but I'm trying—because it's the only way that will work. Meanwhile, the sooner you understand that no one gets rich quick by using secret information, the better.

Myth: **Cash Value life insurance, like Whole Life, will help me retire wealthy.**

Truth: **Cash Value life insurance is one of the worst financial products available.**

No one gets rich quick by using secret information.

Sadly, over 70 percent of the life insurance policies sold today are Cash Value policies. A Cash Value policy is an insurance product that packages insurance and savings together. Do not invest money in life insurance; the returns are horrible. Your insurance person will show you wonderful projections, but none of these policies perform as projected.

Let's look at an example. If a thirty-year-old man has $100 per month to spend on life insurance and shops the top five Cash Value companies, he will find he can purchase an average of $125,000 in insurance for his family. The pitch is to get a policy that will build up savings for retirement, which is what a Cash Value policy does. However, if this same guy purchases twenty-year level term insurance with coverage of $125,000, the cost will be only $7 per month, not $100. Wow. If he goes with the Cash Value option, the other $93 per month should be in savings, right? Well, not really; you see, there are expenses. Expenses? How much? All of the $93 per month disappears in commissions and expenses for the first three years; after that, the return will average 2.6 percent per year for Whole Life, 4.2 percent for Universal Life, and 7.4 percent for the new-and-improved Variable Life policy that includes mutual funds. These statistics are from *Consumer Reports*, Consumer Federation of America, *Kiplinger's Personal Finance*, and *Fortune* magazine, so these are the real numbers.

Worse yet, with Whole Life and Universal Life, the savings you finally build up after being ripped off for years don't go to your family upon your death; the only benefit paid to your family is the face value of the policy, the $125,000 of our example. The truth is that you would be better off to get the $7 term policy and put the extra $93 in a cookie jar! At least after three years you would have $3,000, and when you died your family would get your savings.

As you continue in this book and learn how to have a Total Money Makeover, you will begin investing well. Then, when you are fifty-seven and the kids are grown and gone, the house is paid for, and you have $700,000 in mutual funds, you'll become self-insured. That means when your twenty-year term is up, you shouldn't need life insurance at all— because with no kids to feed, no house payment, and $700,000, your spouse will just have to suffer through if you die without insurance.

Myth: **Playing the Lotto and other forms of gambling will make you rich.**

Truth: **Lotto and Power Ball are a tax on the poor and people who can't do math.**

Just the other day, I was in a Lotto state for a speaking engagement. I went into the gas station to pay for my fill-up and saw a line of people. For a moment I thought I was going to have to stand in line to pay for my gas, before I realized that the line was for purchasing Lotto tickets. Have you ever seen those lines? Next time you do, look at the people in the line. Darryl and his other brother Darryl. These are not rich people, and these are not smart people. The Lotto is a tax on poor people and on people who can't do math. Rich people and smart people would be in the line if the Lotto were a real wealth-building tool, but the truth is that the Lotto is a rip-off instituted by our government. This is not a moral position; it is a mathematical, statistical fact. Studies show that the zip codes that spend four times what anyone else does on lottery tickets are those in lower-income parts of town. The Lotto, or gambling of any kind, offers false hope, not a ticket out. A Total Money Makeover offers hope because it works. Remember, I have been broke twice in my life, but never poor; poor is a state of mind.

> The Lotto is a tax on poor people and on people who can't do math.

Gambling represents false hope and denial. Energy, thrift, and diligence are how wealth is built, not dumb luck.

Myth: Mobile homes, or trailers, will allow me to own something instead of renting, and that will help me to become wealthy.

Truth: Trailers go down in value rapidly, making your chances for wealth building less than if you had rented.

Trailers go down in value rapidly. People who buy a $25,000 double-wide home will in five years owe $22,000 on a trailer worth $8,000. Financially, it's like living in your new car. If I were to suggest you invest $25,000 into a mutual fund with a proven track record of dropping to $8,000 in just five years, you would look at me as if I had lost my mind. I am not above living in a mobile home. I have lived in worse. I just know mobile homes are lousy places to put money. Please don't kid yourself on this. If it walks like a duck and quacks like a duck, it is a duck. Call it "manufactured housing," put it on a permanent foundation, add lots of improvements around the yard, and it is still a trailer when you are ready to sell it.

I want you to own a home because homes are a good investment. The fastest way to become a homeowner is through a Total Money Makeover while renting the cheapest thing you can suffer through. The purchase of a trailer is not a shortcut, but a setback on the path to owning real estate that goes up in value. If the typical consumer considering buying your home can walk up and tell it was ever a trailer in any form, your home will go down, not up, in value.

The only exception to the "no trailers" rule is Ron's plan. Ron graduated from Financial Peace University and was on track for a Total Money Makeover. Ron and his wife prayerfully decided to sell their nice $120,000 home on which they owed only $50,000. They bought a small farm and a very used $3,000 trailer. With no payments and an income of $85,000, they saved and built a very nice, paid-for $250,000 home in just a couple of years. The appraisal was $250,000, but since they paid cash for the land, they got a bargain. Also, as a contractor Ron built the home for pennies on the dollar, so it didn't take them long to finish paying for the home. They sold the $3,000 trailer for $3,200; after all, $3,000 trailers have lost about all their value, so the sale comes down to negotiating.

Myth: **Prepaying my funeral or my kids' college expenses is a good way to invest and protect myself against inflation.**

Truth: **Plans for prepaid funerals and college expenses give low rates of return and put money in the other guy's pocket.**

When you prepay something, your return on investment (interest) is the amount the item will go up in value before you use it. In other words, by prepaying, you avoid the price increases, and that is your return. Prepaying items is like investing at the item's inflation rate. For example, prepaying college tuition will save you the amount tuition goes up between the time you lock in and the time your child begins his college education. The average inflation rate for tuition nationally is about 7 percent, so prepaying tuition is like investing money at 7 percent. That is not bad, but mutual funds will average about 12 percent over a long period of time, and you can save for college tax-FREE. (More about college saving later in your Total Money Makeover.)

The same concept is true for prepaid burial plans. If you have gone through the gut-wrenching exercise of selecting a casket, burial plot, and so on in the middle of grief, you don't want loved ones to experience the same. Preplanning the details of your funeral is wise, but prepaying is unwise. Sara's mom died suddenly, and the grief was overwhelming. In the midst of that pain, Sara felt they made unwise purchases as part of the funeral arrangements, and she vowed not to leave her family in the same predicament. So Sara, age thirty-nine, paid $3,500 for a prepaid funeral. Again, it is wise to preplan, not to prepay. Why? If she were to invest $3,500 in a mutual fund averaging 12 percent, upon an average death age of seventy-eight, Sara's mutual fund would be worth $368,500! I think Sara could be buried for that, with a little left over, unless of course she is King Tut!

Myth: I don't have time to work on a budget, retirement plan, or estate plan.

Truth: You don't have time not to.

Most people concentrate on the urgent in our culture. We worry about our health and focus on our money only after they're gone. Dr. Stephen Covey's book, *The Seven Habits of Highly Effective People,* examines this problem. Dr. Covey says one of the habits of highly effective people is that they begin with the end in mind. Wandering through life aimlessly will bring you much frustration.

> We worry about our health and focus on our money only after they're gone.

Covey says to divide activities into four quadrants. Two of the quadrants are Important/Urgent and Important/Not Urgent. The other two are "Not Important," so let's skip those. We take care of the Urgent/Important stuff, but what is Important/Not Urgent in a Total Money Makeover is planning. You can pay the electric bill or sit in the dark, but if you don't do a monthly spending plan, there is no apparent immediate damage.

John Maxwell has the best quote on budgeting I have ever heard. I wish I had said it: "A budget is people telling their money where to go instead of wondering where it went." You have to make your money behave, and a written plan is the whip and chair for the money tamer.

Earl Nightingale, motivational legend, said that most people spend more time picking out a suit of clothes than planning their careers or even their retirements. What if your life depended on how you managed your 401k or whether you started your Roth IRA today? Actually, it does—because the quality of your life at retirement depends on your becoming an expert in money management today.

Estate planning is never urgent until someone dies. You must think long-term to win with money, and that includes thinking all the way through death. More on this later, but just remember, everyone must budget, plan retirement, and do estate planning—everyone.

Myth: **The debt-management companies on TV, like AmeriDebt, will save me.**

Truth: **You may get out of debt, but only with your credit trashed.**

Debt-management companies are springing up everywhere. These companies "manage" your debt by taking one monthly payment from you and distributing the money among your creditors, with whom they've often worked out lower payments and lower interest. This is not a loan as with debt consolidation. Sometimes people get the two confused. Both are bad, but we have already covered the debt consolidation loans. However, because America needs a Total Money Makeover, the debt management business has become one of the fastest-growing industries today. Companies like AmeriDebt and Consumer Credit Counseling Service can help you get better interest rates and lower payments, but at a price. When you use one of these companies and then try to get a Conventional, FHA, or VA loan, you will be treated the same as if you had filed a Chapter 13 Bankruptcy. Mortgage underwriting guidelines for traditional mortgages will consider your credit trashed, so don't do it.

Another problem with debt management by someone else is that your habits don't change. You can't have someone lose weight for you; you have to change your exercise and diet habits. Handling money is the same way; you have to change your behavior. Turning all your problems over to someone else treats the symptom, not the problem.

Our firm does financial counseling and certifies counselors around the nation for referrals. We will not handle your money for you. We lead you into a mandatory Total Money Makeover. We are not baby-sitters. We have had thousands of clients over the years who have gone to debt-management companies for help. When the clerk taking the order couldn't make the person's life fit their cookie-cutter computer program, the customer was advised to file for bankruptcy. After meeting with them, it was obvious that the customer wasn't bankrupt; they just needed radical surgery. Don't take bankruptcy advice from debt-management companies; you likely aren't bankrupt.

> ## Myths vs. Truth
>
> **Myth:** Everything will be fine when I retire. I know I'm not saving yet, but it will be okay.
>
> **Truth:** Ed McMahon isn't coming.

Of the debt-management companies, Consumer Credit is the best. They do the most thorough job, some branches actually educate, and they are the most powerful in the renegotiation of your debt. You still destroy your credit by using them though, so don't do it; but if I absolutely can't talk you out of it, they are the one to use. AmeriDebt is probably one of the worst. The *Washington Post* reports that Andris Pukke pleaded guilty on two occasions to federal charges of defrauding customers in a debt-consolidation loan scam; that same month "his wife" opened AmeriDebt. AmeriDebt has one of the worst Better Business Report files of any debt-management company, yet last year it spent $15 million on advertising and had gross sales well in excess of $40 million. There is nothing wrong with making money or advertising, but the consumer is being misled, and complaints on this company are through the roof. Stay away.

Myth: **I can buy a kit to clean up my credit, and all my past misdeeds will be washed away.**

Truth: **Only inaccuracies can be cleaned from credit reports, so this is a scam.**

The Federal Fair Credit Reporting Act dictates how consumers and creditors interact with the credit bureaus. Bad credit drops off your credit report after seven years unless you have a Chapter 7 Bankruptcy, which stays on for ten years. Your credit report is your financial reputation, and you can't have anything taken off your report unless the item is inaccurate. If you have an inaccuracy that needs to be removed, see the form letters in the back of this book and do it yourself. Accurate bad credit stays unless you lie. Lying for the purpose of getting money is fraud. Don't do it.

Credit-repair companies are largely scams. The Federal Trade Commission regularly conducts raids to close down these fraudulent companies. I have had many callers on my radio show who purchased a $300 kit to "clean" their credit. Sometimes the kit tells you to dispute all bad credit and ask to have it removed even if the item is reported accurately. Don't do that. The worst idea the kits push is to get a new Social Security number. By getting a second identity, you get a brand-new credit report, and lenders will never know about your past misdeeds. This is fraud, and if you do this, you will go to jail, do not pass go, go directly to jail, fraud. You are lying to get a loan, which is not credit cleanup, and this is criminal.

Clean your credit with a Total Money Makeover. I will show you how

Dave Rants . . .

I am not against the enjoyment of money. What I am against is spending money when you do not have money to begin with.

to live under control, pay cash for stuff so you don't need credit, and over time your credit will clean itself.

Myth: **My divorce decree says my spouse has to pay the debt, so I don't.**

Truth: **Divorce decrees do not have the power to take your name off credit cards and mortgages, so if your spouse doesn't pay, be ready to. You still owe the debt.**

Divorce happens a lot, and it is truly sad. Divorce means we split up everything, including the debts; however, the debts are not easily split. If your name is on a debt, you are liable to pay it, and your credit is affected if you don't. A divorce court does not have the power to take your name off a debt. The divorce judge only has the power to tell your spouse to pay it for you. If your spouse doesn't pay, you can tell the judge, but you are still liable. A lender who doesn't get paid will correctly report bad credit on all parties to the loan, including you. A lender who doesn't get paid can correctly sue the parties to the loan, including you.

If your ex-husband keeps his truck that you both signed for and then doesn't make the payments, your credit is damaged, the truck gets repo'ed, and you will get sued for the balance. If you quitclaim-deed your ownership in the family home to your ex-wife as part of the settlement, you will find yourself in a mess. A quitclaim deed is the easy way to give up ownership in your home. If she doesn't pay on time, your credit is trashed; if she gets foreclosed on, so have you. Even if she pays perfectly on the home or he does on the truck, you will find that you have trouble buying the next home because you have too much debt.

If you are going to leave a marriage, make sure that all debts are refinanced out of your name or force the sale of the item. Don't have the attitude: "I don't want to make him sell his truck." If you are that much in love, don't get divorced; but if you are walking away, make it a complete, clean break even though it's painful now. I have counseled thousands of people who were broken financially by ex-spouses and bad advice from a divorce attorney. So sell the house or refinance it as part of the divorce, period. The only other option is mega risk, and you can count on heartache and even more anger coming your way.

Myth: That collector was so helpful; he really likes me.

Truth: Collectors are not your friends.

There are a few good collectors, very few. Almost every time a collector is "understanding," or wants to "be your friend," there is a reason: to get you to pay your bill. The other technique is to be mean and nasty, and you may find your new "friend" using all kinds of bullying tactics once you have a "relationship."

Your Total Money Makeover will cause you to pay your debts. I want you to pay what you owe, but collectors are not your friends. Credit-card collectors are the worst, for they will lie, cheat, and steal—and that is just before breakfast. You can tell if a credit-card collector is lying by looking to see if his lips are moving. Any deal, special plan, or settlement you make with collectors must be in writing BEFORE you send them money. Otherwise, you will find that you don't have a deal, that they lied. Never allow collectors electronic access to your checking account, and never send postdated checks. They will abuse you if you give them this power, and there will be nothing you can do, because you owe them money. Clear?

Myth: I'll just file bankruptcy and start over; it seems so easy.

Truth: Bankruptcy is a gut-wrenching, life-changing event that causes lifelong damage.

Kathy called my radio show, ready to file bankruptcy. Her debts were overwhelming, and her cheating husband had left with his girlfriend. The house was in his name, as was all the debt except $11,000. Kathy is twenty years old, and her brilliant uncle, a lawyer from California, told her to file bankruptcy. Kathy is beat up, beat down, and deserted, but she is not bankrupt. When her soon-to-be ex-husband ends up with all the debt in his name, he may be bankrupt, but Kathy isn't.

Bankruptcy is not something I recommend any more than I would recommend divorce. Are there times when good people see no way out and file bankruptcy? Yes, but I will still talk you out of it if given the opportunity. Few people who have been through bankruptcy would report that it is a painless wiping-clean of the slate, after which you merrily trot off into your future to start fresh. Don't let anyone fool you. I have been bankrupt and have worked with the bankrupt for decades, and it is not a place you want to visit.

Bankruptcy is listed in the top five life-altering negative events that we can go through, along with divorce, severe illness, disability, and loss of a loved one. I would never say that bankruptcy is as bad as losing a loved one, but it is life-altering and leaves deep wounds both to the psyche and the credit report.

> Bankruptcy is life-altering and leaves deep wounds both to the psyche and the credit report.

Chapter 7 Bankruptcy, which is total bankruptcy, stays on your credit report for ten years. Chapter 13 Bankruptcy, more like a payment plan, stays on your credit report for seven years. Bankruptcy, however, is for life. Loan applications and many job applications ask if you have ever filed for bankruptcy. Ever. If you lie to get a loan because your bankruptcy is very old, technically you have committed criminal fraud.

Most bankruptcies can be avoided with a Total Money Makeover. Your Total Money Makeover may involve extensive amputation of stuff, which will be painful, but bankruptcy is much more painful. If you take the thoughtful step backward to get on solid ground instead of looking at the false allure of the quick fix that bankruptcy seems to offer, you will win more quickly and easily. I know from personal experience the pain of bankruptcy, foreclosure, and lawsuits. Been there, done that, got the T-shirt, and it is not worth it.

We always knew that the debt was bad, but we figured that since we were able to make the payments, it was okay. I remember my husband talking about Dave Ramsey, a guy on the radio, and his Total Money Makeover plan. When Glenn told me that he wanted us to try the plan; I wanted to laugh because Glenn loves to spend money . . . "Bigger, better, faster" was his motto. And we had the bills to prove it.

Well, I figured I could survive trying the plan. Before I knew it, we were having the time of our lives. We found ourselves looking forward to working on the plan. In about thirteen weeks we had dumped $40,000 worth of debt! Two years later, we were debt-free except for the mortgage.

It wasn't long after that when tragedy struck our home. Glenn was diagnosed with a massive tumor, which was so large that the doctors didn't hold much hope. They sent him home and gave him a grim outlook of six months to live and predicted a slow, agonizing death. The doctors may have given up hope, but his family and I never lost our faith.

With no money coming in, I was unable to make our mortgage payment. I contacted the bank and told them of our situation. Foreclosure on the house was inevitable, and the outlook was bleak.

Three long surgeries, six hospitals, and countless doctors later, Glenn was on the road to recovery. It wasn't long after Glenn's surgeries that we started receiving his disability checks. Now that Glenn was doing better, I started agonizing over the bills that were sure to arrive and how much I would still owe on the house after foreclosure. Bankruptcy now seemed inevitable.

Two years have gone by, and our credit rating may have been damaged, but we did not declare bankruptcy. It's funny, but a credit rating isn't very important after you choose to stop borrowing money! The bank bought back the house for what we owed. We kept up with the "ever-challenging" doctors' bills and have managed to continue applying The Total Money Makeover principles. We now have a net worth of just under $80,000!

Things may seem without hope and overwhelming; but learning to put things in order through baby steps, instead of filing bankruptcy, is a must-do!

Glenn (age 41)
and Joann (younger!) Banfield
Computer Consultant;
Shipping

Myth: **I can't use cash because it is dangerous; I might get robbed.**

Truth: **You are being robbed every day by not using the power of cash.**

We teach people to carry cash. In a culture where the salesclerk thinks you are a drug dealer if you pay with cash, I know this suggestion may seem weird. However, cash is powerful. If you carry cash, you spend less, and you can get bargains by flashing cash. Linda e-mailed my newspaper column, complaining that she would get robbed if she carried cash. I explained to her that crooks don't have X-ray vision to look into her pocket or purse. The crooks assume that your purse is like all the others filled with credit cards that are over the limit. Look, I'm not making light of crime. There's a chance you may get robbed, because people do get robbed—whether they carry cash or not. And if it happens to you, the cash will be taken. But, trust me, you need to be far more worried about the danger of using credit cards than the danger of being robbed while carrying cash. Carrying cash doesn't make you more likely to get robbed; on the contrary, the mismanagement of plastic is robbing you every month.

We have already destroyed the myth of credit cards and shown that when you spend cash you spend less. When you put together your written game plan, you will find that managing spending categories as part of your Total Money Makeover is a must to gain control. Cash enables you to say no to yourself. When the food envelope is getting low on cash, we eat leftovers instead of ordering pizza, again.

Myth: I can't afford insurance.

Truth: Some insurance you can't afford to be without.

Today as I went to lunch, I met Steve and Sandy in my reception area. They came by to say thanks. What for? This young couple in their twenties listen to our radio program, and because I constantly push people to get the right kinds of insurance, they did. This year they got term life insurance and a Medical Saving Account health insurance policy. "Good thing we did what you said to do," said Steve as he pulled off his cap to reveal a shaved head with a big scar across the top. "What in the world happened?" I asked. The scar was from a biopsy that revealed inoperable brain cancer. Steve promised he is going to beat it. Sandy smiled and said, "The health insurance has already paid over $100,000 in bills, and we would be sunk if we hadn't followed through as you push all the time." Also, Steve is now uninsurable, so he's thankful to have his term life insurance in place. Our prayers are with this young couple. (Steve's story follows.) By being responsible and buying the right kinds of insurance, they have covered life and death, which we all have to do.

My name is Steven Maness. I'm twenty-eight, I'm debt-free, and I have brain cancer.

I found Dave Ramsey on the radio and became a fan immediately. Growing up, I had accepted debt as a part of life.

At first, I tried to get my wife, Sandy, to buy into The Total Money Makeover plan. To say she was reluctant might be the understatement of the year, especially when she figured out we would have to sell her 2000 Toyota 4Runner to become debt-free. We sat down together and looked at our overall financial picture. We owed about $46,000. We knew we had to change. She started tuning in to Dave, and we started discussing our finances. We agreed to start the "Baby Steps" mentioned in The Total Money Makeover. We simply followed what Dave taught.

It took us twelve months to kill $46,000 in debt. We sold a bunch of "stuff." We moved twice to save money on rent. As Dave would say, we got "gazelle intense." Every sacrifice was worth it. We've never felt more alive!

After becoming debt-free, we were able to give our part-time business a full-time chance. Still following Dave's advice, we opened a Medical Savings Account (MSA) and secured twenty-year term insurance. Along with deciding to become debt-free, the MSA and term insurance have literally saved our lives.

This past year, I was diagnosed with an inoperable form of brain *cancer at the ripe old age of twenty-eight. The MSA that we chose has a $5,000 deductible, but it covers 100 percent of anything above the deductible. My medical bills approached $100,000 within the first two months. The MSA, along with our term insurance, saved our financial lives. Even after I'm gone, I know my beautiful, twenty-three-year-old wife will be taken care of. It's all because of Dave's advice.*

I can't imagine worrying about making payments on $46,000 in debt and worrying about coming up with the cash to cover our part of an 80/20 insurance plan. Or wishing I'd taken the time to set up term insurance to take care of my wife. Thanks to Dave, Sandy and I can stand side by side and fight this fight. With God's help, we will win.

> *Steve (age 28)*
> *and Sandy (age 23) Maness*
> *Self-employed*

We all hate insurance, until we need it. We pay and pay and pay premiums, and sometimes we feel insurance poor. There are certainly many gimmicks in the world of insurance. We cover insurance in detail at Financial Peace University and in other books, but you must have insurance in some basic categories as part of a Total Money Makeover:

> **We all hate insurance, until we need it.**

- Auto and Homeowner Insurance—Choose higher deductibles in order to save on premiums. With high liability limits, these are the best buys in the insurance world.

- Life Insurance—Purchase twenty-year level term insurance equal to about ten times your income. Term insurance is cheap and the only way to go; never use life insurance as a place to save money.

- Long-Term Disability—If you are thirty-two years old, you are twelve times more likely to become disabled than to die by age sixty-five. The best place to buy disability insurance is through work at a fraction of the cost. You can usually get coverage that equals from 50 to 70 percent of your income.

- Health Insurance—The number-one cause of bankruptcy today is medical bills; number two is credit cards. One way to control costs is to look for large deductibles to lower your premium. If you are self-employed, look for an MSA (Medical Savings Account); this type of insurance saves premiums and taxes.

- Long-Term Care Insurance—If you are over sixty, buy Long-Term Care insurance to cover in-home care or nursing home care. The average nursing home stay costs $40,000 per year, which will crack and scramble a nest egg in a heartbeat. Dad in the nursing home can use up Mom's $250,000 savings in just a few short years. Make your parents get it.

I began listening to Dave about ten years ago. At the time, I had graduated from Vanderbilt University with over $60,000 in debt and had done little to attack the principal on this debt.

I recognized the burden of debt since I earned less than $20,000 per year in ministry, and my bills quickly began to pile up, especially my student loans.

Besides the $65,000 in student-loan debt, I had several hundred in hospital bills; soon some very angry creditors began calling. I *got married, assumed about $12,000 of my wife's credit-card debt, and adopted my wife's daughter. After three months of marriage, my ministry job ended, and I was without employment with a new family. If that weren't enough, my wife and I found out we were pregnant.*

In the past five years, under the arduous circumstances of no job, high debt, a new wife and family, pregnancy, and no insurance, I was continually encouraged by my faith and by listening to The Dave Ramsey Show *on the radio. I did not seek the help of credit cards to get me out of this mess!*

I eventually landed a job in medical software sales and immediately got some health insurance. Our son was born later that year. Through a series of unfortunate circumstances, our son was diagnosed with cancer a year later. He had many surgeries and ultimately went to heaven in the same year. I mention this because of the importance of health insurance. If we did not have it, we easily could have been in debt for several hundred thousand dollars! Through the generosity of the people around us, we did not have much debt, but we had the pain of losing our first son. Only through Jesus and our church did we come through this.

Health insurance is a must!

> *Scott Kozimor (age 34)*
> *Sales Director*

Myth: **If I do a will, I might die.**

Truth: **You are going to die—so do it with a will.**

Estate planners tell us that 70 percent of Americans die without a will. Dumb, really dumb. The state, known for its financial prowess, will decide what happens to your stuff, your kids, and your financial legacy. The proverb says, "A good man leaves an inheritance to his children's children" (Prov. 13:22 NKJV). I am a pragmatist, and so I don't understand all the fretting over a will. A will is a gift you leave your family or loved ones. It is a gift because it makes the management of your estate very clear and light-years easier.

SHOCKING STATS

70% of Americans die without a will.

You are going to die, so go out in style, and die with a will in place.

We've revealed Debt Myths and Money Myths. If you have carefully read and understood why these myths are untrue, I have great news for you. Your Total Money Makeover has already begun! The Total Money Makeover is a remaking of your view of money so that you permanently change how you deal with money. You must walk to the beat of a different drummer, the same beat that the wealthy hear. If the beat sounds common or normal, evacuate the dance floor immediately. The goal is not to be normal because, as my radio listeners know by now, normal is broke.

5

Two More Hurdles:
Ignorance and Keeping Up with the Joneses

Denial (I don't have a problem), Debt Myths (debt is how you become wealthy), and Money Myths (stories told by the culture) are three major obstacles that keep you from becoming a fiscally fit body of money management and staying power. Before we move to the proven plan, we must explore two more enemies of your Total Money Makeover.

If you have a major issue with Ben and Jerry's Ice Cream, you should tell your trainer before you try to change your diet and exercise program. First, you must admit your ice-cream problem and recognize the myths about ice cream as a great weight-loss product. The point is, we must identify the enemy, the hurdles to winning. To set out a game plan and not acknowledge the obstacles to that plan would be immature and unrealistic. Those of us who have been knocked around by life know that we must find the problems or obstacles and plan a way over them, through them, or around them. If you can box up the things that would defeat your Total Money Makeover, then the plan will work. The first step to losing weight and toning up is to identify weight-loss myths, overeating, wrong eating, and no exercise as problems to overcome; the same is true for a Total Money Makeover. As the great

> "We have met the enemy and he is us."

77

philosopher Pogo from the Sunday comics said years ago, "We have met the enemy and he is us."

Hurdle #1: Ignorance: No One Is Born Financially Smart

The first hurdle is Ignorance. In a culture that worships knowledge, to say ignorance about money is an issue makes some people defensive. Don't be defensive. Ignorance is not lack of intelligence; it is lack of know-how. I have seen many newborn babies of friends, relatives, church members, and team members. I have never seen a baby that was born ready to be wealthy. Never do the friends and relatives gather around the window of the nursery and exclaim, "Oh, look! She is a born financial genius!"

No one is born with the knowledge of how to drive a car. We are taught the skill (although some of us don't seem to have learned). No one is born with the knowledge of how to read and write; we are taught how. None of these are innate skills; all must be taught. Likewise, no one is born with the knowledge of how to handle money, but we AREN'T taught that!

> Ignorance is not lack of intelligence; it is lack of know-how.

At the coffeepot one day, one of my leaders said, "We need to get this Total Money Makeover process taught in college." Before she could graduate from a small Christian college, she was required to take a class on how to interview and hunt for a job. She said the class wasn't very hard academically, but its practical implications made it one of the most valuable classes she took in college. We go to school to learn to earn; we earn, and then have no idea what to do with the money. According to the Census Bureau, the average family in America last year made $40,816. Even if they never get a raise, the average family will make over $2 million in a working lifetime! And we teach NOTHING about how to manage this money in most high schools and colleges. We graduate from school and go out into the world and get a financial master's degree in D.U.M.B.

Do we make a mess of our finances because we aren't intelligent? No. If you put someone who has never driven a car, has never seen a car, and can't spell *car,* in the driver's seat of a brand-new car, the wreck will come before leaving the driveway. Backing up and gaining more speed only leads to another wreck. "Trying harder" isn't the answer because the next wreck will not only total the car but also hurt other people. This is ludicrous!

During our lifetimes we make $2 million, yet we graduate from high school, college, or even graduate school and can't spell *financial.* This is a bad plan! We have quit teaching personal finance, and we have to start again. That is why Financial Peace for the Next Generation is taught in high

Dave Rants . . .

Stupid things are always going to be done in families unless the wiser member learns to stand up to the forceful one.

schools around the nation; however, our high-school curriculum won't help you unless you are still in high school.

If you made a mess of your money and/or haven't gotten the best use from it, usually the reason is that you were never taught to do so. Ignorance doesn't mean dumb; it means you have to learn how. I'm fairly intelligent. I have had multiple best-selling books, speak to millions on my radio program, and run a multimillion-dollar company, but if you asked me to work on your car, I would make a mess. I don't know how; I'm ignorant in that area.

Overcoming ignorance is easy. First, with no shame, admit that you are not a financial expert because you were never taught. Second, finish this book. Third, go on a lifetime quest to learn more about money. You don't need to apply to Harvard to get an MBA with a specialization in finance; you don't have to watch the financial channel instead of a great movie.

You do need to read something about money at least once a year. You should occasionally attend a seminar about money. Your actions should show that you care about money by learning something about it.

Sharon and I have a great marriage—not perfect, but great. Why? We read about marriage, we go to marriage retreat weekends, we date weekly, we sometimes take a Sunday school class on marriage, and we even meet once in a while with a friend who is a Christian marriage counselor. Do we do all these things because our marriage is weak? No, we do all these things to make our marriage great. We have a great marriage because we work at it, make it a priority, and seek knowledge on marriage. Great marriages don't just happen. Wealth doesn't just happen. You will spend some time and effort on getting rid of ignorance. Again, you do not need to become a financial geek; you just need to spend more time on your 401k options and your budget than you do picking out this year's vacation.

I started listening to Dave Ramsey on the radio a little over two years ago and also attended a live speaking event. I was so impressed and motivated that I enrolled in Financial Peace University. I was eight months pregnant, and we had just under $340,000 in debt. My dream was to be a stay-at-home mom, but that seemed impossible. My husband made only $36,000 a year.

My husband, who had wanted nothing to do with the finances because he would then have to be responsible, really enjoyed the plan. I think we both realized that we needed to be together in this.

We canceled unnecessary services; looked into how we spent our money, and sold an SUV and a sports car to purchase one reliable midsize car. We had rented out the first house that we owned and were living in the second, the one we bought for retirement. We sold the second house and made a budget, started successfully using envelopes, and began paying off everything that we could.

We are not out of debt yet, but we're definitely on the road. We gave up many things, but we feel more mature and less stressed because of it. I am happy to say that we have paid down our debt to approximately $150,000 in two short years. We cut up more than twenty-eight credit cards. We have just moved back to our first house, so our monthly bills are much less, and we can start to tackle the rest of the debt.

My husband calls Dave and The Total Money Makeover plan "the guy with the plan that made us give up our house but saved our marriage"!

Christina Curtis (age 33)
Homemaker

Ignorance is not okay. "What you don't know won't hurt you" is a really stupid statement. What you don't know will kill you. What you don't know about money will make you broke and keep you broke. Finish this book and read others. You can always check my Web site at daveramsey.com for recommended reading by other authors that generally line up with my teachings.

Hurdle #2: Keeping Up with the Joneses: The Joneses Can't Do Math

The second hurdle in this chapter is Keeping Up with the Joneses. Peer pressure, cultural expectations, "reasonable standard of living"—I don't care how you say it, we all need to be accepted by our crowd and our families. This need for approval and respect drives us to do some really insane things. One of the paradoxically dumb things we do is to destroy our finances by buying garbage we can't afford to try to make ourselves appear wealthy to others. Dr. Tom Stanley wrote a wonderful book in the '90s that you should read entitled *The Millionaire Next Door*. His book is a study of America's millionaires. Remember, if you want to be thin and muscular, you should study the habits of people who are thin and muscular. If you want to be rich, you should study the habits and value systems of the rich. In his study of millionaires, Stanley discovered that the habits and value systems were not what most people think. When we think of millionaires, we think of big houses, new cars, and really nice clothes. Stanley found that most million-

> ## Dum Math & Stupid Tax
>
> ### Get a Head Start on Big-Time Debt
>
> The average college student pays $5,000 *more per year* to live and eat off-campus than to live in the dorm and eat cafeteria food. Student loans were needed not to earn their degree but only to look good while getting it.

aires don't have those things. He found the typical millionaire lives in a middle-class home, drives a two-year-old or older paid-for car, and buys blue jeans at Wal-Mart. In short, Stanley found that the typical million-aire found infinitely more motivation from the goal of financial security than from what friends and family think. The need for approval and respect from others based on what they own was virtually nonexistent.

If we look at Stanley's findings and hold those up against Ken and Barbie's life plan, we find Ken and Barbie to be lost, off course, and clueless. Ken and Barbie are in our office all the time for financial counseling. Last year they were here, and their names were Bob and Sara. Bob and Sara make $93,000 per year and have for the last seven years. What do they have to show for it? A $400,000 home that they still owe $390,000 on, including a home equity loan used to furnish it. They have two $30,000 fleeced cars and $52,000 in credit-card debt, but they have traveled well and dressed in high fashion. The $25,000 left on a student loan from college ten years ago is still outstanding because they have no money. On the positive side, they have $2,000 in savings and $18,000 in their 401k. These people have a negative net worth, but they really look good. Bob's mom is very impressed, and Sara's brother frequently stops by to ask for money because they are "obviously doing well." They present the perfect picture of the American dream that has turned into a nightmare. Behind the perfect hair and the French manicure, there was deep desperation, a sense of futility, an unraveling marriage, and disgust with themselves.

> Don't even consider keeping up with the Joneses. THEY'RE BROKE!

This may be one of the places our metaphor of weight loss for fiscal fitness breaks down. If your body were in the same condition that Bob and Sara's money is in, everyone would think, *Five hundred pounds is just too fat.* Your problem would be apparent to family, friends, strangers, and even you. The difference with Bob and Sara is that they have a "dirty little secret." The secret is that they are nowhere near as cool as they appear. They are broke and desperate, and no one knows it. Not only does no one know it, but everyone thinks the opposite is true. So when my counselor made suggestions to turn around this bankruptcy looking for a place to happen, there was more than one place of resistance in the heart. The truth is that Bob and Sara are broke. They need to get rid of the cars and sell the house.

Resistance of the heart is real. First, of course, we like our nice houses and nice cars, and selling them would be painful. Second, we don't want to admit to everyone we have impressed that we are fakes. Yes, when you buy a big pile of stuff with no money and lots of debt, you are a financial fake. Peer pressure is very, very powerful. "We are scaling down" is a painful statement to make to friends or family. "We will have to pass on that trip or dinner because it is not in our budget" is virtually impossible for some people to say. Being real takes tremendous courage. We like approval, and we like respect, and to say otherwise is another form of denial. To wish for the admiration of others is normal. The problem is that this admiration can become a drug. Many of you are addicted to this drug, and the destruction to your wealth and financial well-being caused by your addiction is huge.

> Radical change
> . . . is required
> for a money
> breakthrough.

Radical change in the quest for approval, which has involved purchasing stuff with money we don't have, is required for a money breakthrough. Sara's breakthrough came with family. Her family was upper-middle-crust and had always given Christmas gifts to every member. With twenty nieces and nephews and six sets of adults to buy for, just on her side, the budget was ridiculous. Sara's announcement at Thanksgiving that this year Christmas giving was going to be done with the drawing of names, because she and Bob couldn't afford it, was earth-shattering. Some of you are grinning as if this is no big deal. It was a huge deal in Sara's family! Gift giving was a tradition! Her mother and two of her sisters-in-law were furious. Very little thanks were given that Thanksgiving, but Sara stood her ground and said, "No more."

Sara has a master's degree in sociology, so she is no pushover. She understood how the family dynamic would be upset, and she understood that she would lose approval, admiration, and respect. Sara said later that while she grasped intellectually what her announcement meant, and she knew emotionally and financially that this was the correct thing to do, the reality was very hard. Stong peer pressure from her family literally kept her awake the whole night before. She told me, "As I lay in the dark, I was afraid like a little twelve-year-old girl yearning for approval from her daddy." The courage to address what may seem like a small issue was a huge breakthrough for Sara. That Thanksgiving her heart had a Total Money Makeover, and she was not going to be led into well-dressed poverty by peer pressure anymore.

Ten years ago, my husband and I got married, bought a new house, and completely furnished and landscaped it, all within one year. Forget trying to keep up with the Joneses—we were going to be the Joneses! Next, my husband got a new Chevy truck, and I was the proud owner of a brand-new Corvette. By the following year, we had about fifteen "top of the line" credit cards, and we accumulated about $30,000 in debt by the time all was said and done. We even flew to Vegas for a weekend trip and ended up buying a time-share. We put it on the credit card, of course! But once we came back, we changed our minds about the time-share; we figured we couldn't really afford the payment, and the Corvette was more important. So we paid $2,000 to get out of the time-share. Guess what? We put that on the card, too!

I was also a shopping queen! I could be blindfolded in a mall, and I would still know my way around the stores. We had the best jewelry and clothes that our credit cards could buy! Finally, we were at the point that we had to pay one credit card with another, and we eventually filed for bankruptcy. Our net worth was a negative $140,000, if you counted the house.

Then, out of divine intervention I think, I found Dave Ramsey on the radio. I would listen and laugh most of the time because I knew he was talking to me. You start to see the messes you've made, and then you start to panic. I didn't want us to be eating dog food at age sixty-five and sixty-seven because we were too stupid at thirty-five and thirty-seven!

We started The Total Money Makeover program this past year. We did a budget, and in three years and ten months, we will have paid off $32,500 in car debt and credit cards and have $20,000 for the emergency fund. We will succeed because we are breaking the cycle! We will never, ever, ever again be in that situation because we are SICK AND TIRED OF BEING SICK AND TIRED! Don't even consider keeping up with the Joneses. THEY'RE BROKE!

Tabitha Williams (age 35)
Executive Assistant

Everyone has a weak spot like Sara's. It could be your third-generation failing business that needs to be closed. It could be your clothes shopping. It probably is your car. It could be the boat. Maybe yours is giving to your grown children. Unless you have had a heart-level Total Money Makeover somewhere, sometime, in your life, you are still doing something with money to impress others, and that has to change before you can get on a real plan to fiscal fitness. The Bible states, "Godliness with contentment is great gain" (1 Tim. 6:6 NKJV). Those of us who have had a Total Money Makeover still know where our Achilles heel is and still see that weak spot as a fatal wound if we allow it to grow again. What is the one "money thing" that makes you grin inside when you see others admiring it? Do you need to give it up to break that feeling inside you? Until you recognize that weak area, you will always be prone to financial stupidity on that subject.

My weak spot is cars. After starting with nothing and becoming a millionaire the first time by age twenty-six, I had the eye of my heart set on a Jaguar. I "needed" a Jaguar. What I needed was for people to be impressed with my success. What I needed was family raising an eyebrow of approval based on my ability to win. What I yearned for was respect. What I was so shallow to believe was that the car I drove gave me those things. God used the whole story of what I drove to give my heart a Total Money Makeover in the area of peer pressure.

Totally Broke and Driving a Jag!

As I was going broke, losing everything, I kept the Jaguar by refinancing it repeatedly at different, friendlier banks. I even went so far as to get a good friend to co-sign a loan so I could keep this image car. I couldn't afford to keep up the maintenance on the car, so it began to deteriorate. It ran poorly and wasn't reliable, but I still loved it and hung on. Within the year of our bankruptcy, we were so broke that our electricity was once cut off for two days. I have often wondered what the guy from the electric company thought as he stood in the driveway next to my Jaguar and pulled my electric meter. That is sick. The car continued to deteriorate, and the main seal on the oil pan cracked. This caused oil coming out the back of the engine onto the muffler to burn. The burning oil, lots of it, created a smoke screen for miles behind me everywhere I went. The bid to fix it was $1,700, and I hadn't seen an extra $1,700 in months, so I just kept driving my James Bond smoke-screen-mobile. Finally, my friend got really tired of making the payments he had co-signed for and gently suggested I sell my precious car. I was mad at him. How dare he suggest that I sell my car! So he quit making the payments, and the bank not so gently suggested I sell the car or they

> **Myths vs. Truth**
>
> **Myth:** Car payments are a way of life; you'll always have one.
>
> **Truth:** Staying away from car payments by driving reliable used cars is what the average millionaire does; that is how he or she became a millionaire.

would repo it. I tried to stall and only came to my senses and sold the Jaguar on a Thursday morning because the bank assured me they would take it on Friday. I was able to work my way through the mess, pay the bank and even my friend back, but the process was humiliating. Because I was too stubborn to address what that car represented in my life, I caused much damage that was avoidable.

An interesting footnote about how healing can occur on your weak spot: I was so disgusted with myself when I woke up and realized the depth of my stupidity that I swore off my drug, cars. I went to abstinence, meaning I didn't care what we drove or what it looked like as long as we were winning in our Total Money Makeover. Fast-forward fifteen years. We had become wealthy again, and I decided to get a different car. I'm always looking for a one- or two-year-old car, I'm always paying cash, and I'm always looking for a deal, not really caring what car it is. I was kind of looking for a Mercedes or a Lexus, but I was really looking for a steal. A friend in the car business called me with a deal—on a Jaguar. So all those years and tears later when it was no longer the driving force of my approval rating, God allowd a Jaguar back into my life. He returned what the locusts had eaten, but He only did so when it was not my idol. Rumor has it that God doesn't like us to have other gods in our lives.

The first time I heard of Dave Ramsey was on the radio. I thought the concepts he was teaching were right, but I did not live by those concepts. I was too busy buying STUFF. Yep, I had what Dave calls "stuffitis"!

I found out that there was a cure for "stuffitis" a couple of years later when a friend and I saw Dave Ramsey at one of his live events. At that time, I had approximately $45,000 in total debt. I had lots of stuff! I had a new Honda Accord and a big-screen television with an awesome sound system that I had bought on fifteen months same as cash. After hearing Dave speak, I knew we had to sell some things and get out of our debt. I had to give up my "stuff," at least for now.

Over the next three years I really decided to follow the Baby Step principles in The Total Money Makeover. I had a budget every month, lived on CASH, and cut up all my credit cards. I sold my new car, the big screen, and the stereo system. During those three years, however, I also got married and went on a seven-day cruise to the Eastern Caribbean with cash!

My wife and I are now debt-free—except for our home. Dave and his principles have truly changed my life.

By the way, we now have a big-screen TV again, one that we bought with cash!

Charles (age 32)
and Andra Bledsoe
Bank Branch Manager;
Stay-at-Home Mom

So maybe someday Sara and Bob will be able to pay cash to take Sara's whole family on a cruise for Christmas. After their Total Money Makeover, Bob and Sara will be able to pay cash for a huge event like that and not even dent their wealth. They will be able to buy that cruise in memory of that fateful Thanksgiving when Sara's heart had a Total Money Makeover in her need for her family's approval. That change has taught Sara and Bob that if they will live like no one else, later they will be able to live like no one else.

Past the Obstacle Course and Up the Mountain

One thing I have learned as I have lost fat, become toned, and generally gotten into better shape is this: Things that require physical output are easier for me. Things like mountain climbing or obstacle courses are actually doable now, not a dream as they were when I was overweight and out of shape. The same is true of our Total Money Makeover journey to fiscal fitness. Have you realized by now that the start of your Total Money Makeover is almost an obstacle course? We busted through denial. We waded through and climbed over Debt Myths. We carefully scaled the wall of Money Myths. We are working through Ignorance. And we have learned not to place so much emphasis on our competition on the course; we have permanently quit keeping up with the Joneses, because the Joneses are broke. The obstacle course, however, was only part of our journey.

> ### SHOCKING STATS
>
> 75% of airline miles "rewarded" are never redeemed.

Now we stand at the bottom of a mountain with a clear view of the top. We are in better shape now for mountain climbing, and there are no blind spots. We are ready to climb. The goal is far off, but we can see it clearly now. There is a distinct and very clear path we will take to the top. The good thing about this path is that it is not virgin territory; it is a well-worn path. It is a narrow path, one that most people don't follow, but many winners have. Tens of thousands have followed this path once they made it through the obstacle course.

Take a look back before we start. The climb will be hard, but it will be near impossible if you are still struggling with any of the obstacles. If you are still hanging on to Myths, Denial, or any other obstacles. On this mountain climb you will feel as if you have bricks in your backpack. A couple of pounds of denial might not be fatal, but mixing it with three pounds of "I still think credit cards are good" and a can or two of "folding to peer pressure" will result in a backpack load that will ensure your climb is a failure. Most of us make the first climb wearing a hat of Ignorance, and while it will slow the climb, ignorance will not keep anyone from the top when mixed with some humility. This mountain is doable, but not if you are still bogged down on the obstacle course. Some things I'll tell you to do won't work and will cause damage if you still cling to Denial, Myths, Ignorance, or Approval.

Decide before the climb if you are going to follow the guide. If you aren't going to listen to the seasoned guide who has personally made this climb alone and then returned to lead tens of thousands up this path, then you climb at your own peril. Finish reading the book even if you don't agree with me, but following these steps while trying to hold on to Myths, Ignorance, Approval, or Denial will make your climb very hard and may injure you.

> "Continuing to do the same thing over and over again and expecting a different result is the definition of insanity."

Why not climb? The only other path is to follow all the normal people who are broke. That isn't a path; it is a well-beaten interstate highway. Most people drive around and around, occasionally glancing forlornly at the mountain we will climb, but when they see how tough the obstacle course is just to get to the bottom, those sad souls quit before they ever begin.

The Twelve Steppers have it right. They say, "Continuing to do the same thing over and over again and expecting a different result is the definition of insanity." What you have falsely believed and acted on or not acted on has brought you to the place you are today with your money. If you want to be in a different place, you must believe and do things differently. If I want a smaller waist size than fifty-two inches, I must eat and exercise differently. The change will be painful, but the result will be worth it.

I've been to the top of Total Money Makeover Mountain, and I've led countless others there. I say, IT IS WORTH THE EFFORT! So lace up your shoes of resolve, wave good-bye to your "normal" friends, and let's climb!

6

Save $1,000 Fast:
Walk Before You Run

In my first book, *Financial Peace,* there is a chapter entitled "Baby Steps," the premise of which is that we can do anything financially if we do it one little step at a time. I have developed the Baby Steps over years of counseling one-on-one, in small group discussions, with real-world lives in Financial Peace University, and by answering questions on our radio show. Tens of thousands have followed this tried-and-true system to achieve their Total Money Makeover. The term "baby steps" comes from the comedy *What About Bob?* starring Bill Murray. Bill plays a crazy guy who drives his psychiatrist crazy. The therapist has written a book called *Baby Steps.* The statement "You can get anywhere if you simply go one step at a time" is the framework for the movie. We will use the Baby Steps to walk through our Total Money Makeover. Why do the Baby Steps work? I thought you would never ask.

> "You can get anywhere if you simply go one step at a time."

Eating an Elephant Gives You Energy

The way you eat an elephant is one bite at a time. Find something to do and do that with vigor until it is complete; then and only then do you move to the next step. If you try to do everything at once, you will fail. If you woke up this morning and realized you needed to lose 100 pounds, build your cardiovascular system, and tone your muscles, what would you do? If on the first day of your new plan you quit eating, run three miles, and lift all the weight you can lift with every muscle group, you will collapse. If you don't collapse the first day, wait forty-eight hours for the muscle groups to lock up and the cardio to go crazy, and you will be bingeing on food shortly thereafter. When I went on a quest for a better body and better health a few years ago, my wise trainer didn't try to kill me the first day. Not even by the second week were we pushing the envelope, because he knew I had to create some muscle tone before we could hit hard workouts. We walked before we ran. Plus, if I had tried to do everything at once, I would have been overwhelmed and frustrated with my inability to do it all.

The power of focus is what causes our Baby Steps to work. When you try to do everything at once, progress can be very slow. When you put 3 percent in your 401k, $50 extra on the house payment, and $5 extra on the credit card, you dilute your efforts. Because you attack several areas at once, you don't *finish* anything you start for a long time. That makes you feel that you aren't accomplishing anything, which is very dangerous. If you feel that nothing is getting done, you will soon lose energy for the task of money management altogether. The power of focus is that it works. Things happen. You check stuff off your list. Life gives you an "attaboy" in the form of actual visible progress.

The power of priority also causes the Baby Steps to work. Each of these steps is part of the proven plan to financial fitness I promised you. They build on one another; therefore, if done out of order, they do not work. Think of a 350-pound person beginning marathon training with a quick ten-mile run. The results of not building up to that run could be total frustration at best and a heart attack at worst. So do the Baby Steps in order. Walk around the block and lose some weight before going on a ten-mile run.

To start the Baby Steps, we will work on one important step to the exclusion of others. Patience! We will climb the whole mountain, but not until we first have a strong base camp. You will be tempted to short-circuit the process because you are more concerned about one certain area of your money, but don't do it. These steps are the proven plan to financial fitness, and they are in the right order for everyone. For example, if you are fifty-five with no retirement, you may be tempted to jump to Step Four (Invest 15 Percent of Your Income in Retirement), because you are scared about not being able to retire with dignity. The paradox is that by shortcutting the process, you are much more likely to fail at retiring with dignity. Failure could also occur when you cash out your newly formed retirement plan to cover the inevitable emergency. If you have kids heading toward college, you may be panicking about saving for college, which is covered in Baby Step Five, but don't do it out of order. I will address the problems you'll run into at each stage if you get things out of order, because I have seen most of them. Focus exclusively on the Baby Step you are on even though it seems to be a temporary detriment to other areas of money. Things will be fine if you don't focus on retirement for a few months, as long as you can kick retirement into the stratosphere when we get there.

YOU, Inc.

This chapter is about the first Baby Step, but before we discuss saving $1,000 fast, we need to look at some basic tools needed to win and some ongoing things you should be doing as you go. The dreaded B word enters the picture here. You must set up a budget, a written budget, every month. This is a book about a process that will enable you to win with your money, a process that others have completed successfully, and I assure you that virtually none of the thousands of winners I have seen did so without a written budget.

I had about $30,000 in consumer debt, was recently divorced, and teetered on the verge of bankruptcy four years ago. But now I'm wiser, remarried, and DEBT-FREE!

It wasn't easy. First, I tried to do it on my own. I quit using my credit cards and wasn't building up more debt, but I didn't know how to budget. I kept running out of money before the month was over. I was so ashamed of not being able to pay all my bills that I became physically ill. This affected my new marriage, my job, and my whole life.

Then I started The Total Money Makeover plan.

One of the most important things I learned was to create a "cash-flow" plan, which means spending every penny of what you make on paper before the month begins. You know exactly how much you have to spend on food, gas, clothing, and entertainment. Plus, you know how much you can afford to blow. I like the fact that the book says everyone needs some "blow money," so you just include it in the budget. I put the cash for each category in envelopes and know that is all I can spend.

My husband and I went without a lot of "wants" and haven't taken many vacations in the past few years, but we are out of debt now and excited about our future.

Pam (age 41)
and Scott (age 38) Raney
Nurse; Carpenter

In Chapter 4 on Money Myths, the importance of a written budget was discussed. If you worked for a company called YOU, Inc., and your job at YOU, Inc., was to manage money—and you managed money at YOU, Inc., the way you manage your own money now, would YOU, Inc., fire you? You have to tell money what to do or it leaves. A written budget for the month is your money goal. People who win at anything have written goals. Goals are what you are aiming at. Zig Ziglar says, "If you aim at nothing you will hit it every time." Money won't behave unless you tame it. P. T. Barnum said, "Money is an excellent slave and a horrible master." You wouldn't build a house without a blueprint, so why do you spend your lifetime income of over $2 million without a blueprint? Jesus said, "Which of you, intending to build a tower, does not sit down first and count the cost, whether he has enough to finish it . . ." (Luke 14:28 NKJV).

> **You have to tell money what to do or it leaves.**

I was looking at $60,000 in credit debt over and above my mortgage.

This debt was accumulated mostly over the last five years because we have two daughters who went to college one year apart and then two weddings one and a half years apart! We incurred almost $150,000 in debt. My wife had back surgery twice over the past eight years, and I did not want her ever to have to work again. We rely on my income solely, and this debt hanging over my head every day was like an anvil around my neck. We made minimum payments on just about everything, but we could not keep up! When I took a hard look at my debt picture, I realized that if I continued *making minimum payments, it would take me another forty-five years to pay everything off!*

Obviously, this was not acceptable and not a legacy that I wanted to leave behind. I worked up a budget as suggested in The Total Money Makeover and began the journey to freedom. In about eight months we have paid off over $37,000 in debt and are on track to paying off the card and consumer debt by next year! We have $46,000 left on the mortgage, and that will be paid off in less than two more years!

Since I'm analytic, I created a spreadsheet on my computer to keep track of the progress as well as to generate our monthly budget. It's incredibly exciting to watch the progress each month as we work toward financial freedom. The plan has given us hope not only for today but also for our future. I know that when we are out of debt at age forty-nine, we can take that money we paid someone else and put it to work for us. There will be no cards, no debt, no sleepless nights worrying about the future, just peace of mind knowing that we will be debt-free soon.

> *Paul (age 48)*
> *and Jane (age 46) Anzaldi*
> *Systems Engineer;*
> *Restaurant Owner*

Brian Tracy, motivational speaker, says, "What does it take to succeed on a big scale? A tremendous God-given talent? Inherited wealth? A decade of postgraduate education? Connections? Fortunately for most of us, what it takes is something very simple and accessible: clear, written goals." According to Brian Tracy, a study of Harvard graduates found that after two years, the 3 percent who had written goals achieved more financially than the other 97 percent combined!

This is not a textbook on money; this is a book on the steps to take and how to take them. This isn't a chapter on budgeting; however, many of our budget forms from the Financial Peace software program are in the back of this book for you to use. The instructions are on each page, but let me give you a couple of guidelines to get started on budgeting.

> Income minus outgo equals zero every month.

Set up a new budget every month. Don't try to have the perfect budget for the perfect month because we never have those. Spend every dollar on paper before the month begins. Give every dollar of your income a name before the month begins, which is called a zero-based budget. Income minus outgo equals zero every month. Look at this month's income and this month's bills, savings, and debts, and match them up until you have given every income dollar an outgo name. If you have an irregular income due to commissions, self-employment, or bonuses, use the Irregular-Income Planning sheet in the system to create a prioritized spending plan, but you still must do a written budget before each month begins.

I have had an awesome experience with The Total Money Makeover in my life. I am a single grandmother, raising three of my four grandsons. Before I started the plan, I had a terrible time trying to figure out where I spent my money. I was always stressed over my bills and never seemed to have enough for everything that I needed to pay. It was extremely nerve-racking trying to get all my bills covered and still have money for essentials.

With The Total Money Makeover, I now write out my budget before the first of the month and plan where my money will be spent. Within a year or so, since I finished learning the plan, I *became faithful in writing out my budget each month. I won't say I have never messed up. A couple of times I forgot to write down an annual item (like car tags, insurance), but I was always able to cover it because all my other bills were paid up to date. I have approximately $2,400 saved toward paying off the last of my debts (except my house).*

I have had great peace of mind over my finances. I have been able to tithe according to the Bible. I now also have time to work on other areas of my life that have been left in disarray because I spent all my time (and worry and prayers) on my finances. I believe I will continue to use the envelope system the rest of my life. I will always be grateful to Dave Ramsey for sharing The Total Money Makeover with me.

Patty Patterson (age 49)
Single Mom and Grandmom

Agree on It

If you're married, agree on the budget with your spouse. This one sentence requires a stand-alone book to describe how, but the bottom line is this: If you aren't working together, it is almost impossible to win. Once the budget is agreed on and is in writing, pinky-swear and spit-shake that you will never do anything with money that is not on that paper. The paper is the boss of the money, and you are the boss of what goes on the paper, but you have to stick to the budget, or it's just an elaborate theory.

If something comes up in the middle of the month that causes the budget to need changing, call an emergency budget committee meeting. You can change the budget (and what you do with money) only if you do two things. One, both spouses agree to the change. Two, you must still balance your budget. If you increase what you are spending on car repairs by $50, you must lower what you are spending somewhere else by $50 so that your income minus your outgo still equals zero. This process of mid-course adjustment doesn't have to be a big hairy deal, but both guidelines must be met. You still zero out so you don't blow the budget, and you get spousal approval so you haven't broken the spit pact.

Adriennnne!

Before we get to Baby Step One, you will have to do one other thing. You will have to be current with all your creditors. If you are behind on payments, the first goal will be to become current. If you are far behind, do necessities first, which are basic food, shelter, utilities, clothing, and transportation. Only when you're current with the necessities can you catch up on credit cards and student loans. If you need more help with this level of financial crisis, check our Web site for how to contact one of our certified counselors or order the book *Financial Peace*.

Focused intensity is required to win. I can't stress enough that people who have had a Total Money Makeover, those noted in this book and others across America, got mad. They got sick and tired of being sick and tired! They said, "I've had it!" and went ballistic to change their

> ### Dum Math & Stupid Tax
>
> **It's a Life-and-Life Situation**
>
> Looking to spend $100 per month on life insurance? You could pay $7 a month toward term insurance and invest the remaining $93. But go with a cash-value policy if you'd rather have someone else earn interest on your investments.

lives. There is no intellectual exercise where you can academically work your way into wealth; you have to get fired up. Play the music from *Rocky* in the background and listen for Rocky's cry, "Adriennnne!" Go get 'em, champ! There is no energy in logic; this is behavior and motivation modification, and it works!

After you are current, have a written, agreed-on plan, have the obstacle course behind you, and are focused and intense, you are ready to follow the right priorities. Here we go.

Baby Step One:
Save $1,000 Cash as a Starter Emergency Fund

It *is* going to rain. You need a rainy-day fund. You need an umbrella. *Money* magazine says that 78 percent of us will have a major negative event in a given ten-year period of time. The job is downsized, right-sized, reorganized, or you just plain get fired. There's an unexpected pregnancy: "We weren't going to have kids yet/another one." Car blows up. Transmission goes out. You bury a loved one. Grown kids move home again. Life happens, so be ready. This is not a surprise. You need an emergency fund, an old-fashioned Grandma's rainy-day fund. Sometimes people tell me I should be more positive. Well, I *am* positive; it *is* going to rain, so you need a rainy-day fund. Now, obviously, $1,000 isn't going to catch all these big things, but it will catch the little ones until the emergency fund is fully funded.

> They got sick and tired of being sick and tired! They said, "I've had it!"

We were going nowhere fast financially. Well, actually we were going backward fast. It wasn't a salary issue, since we both had good jobs. It was a spending issue. I was too good at it. We found ourselves nearing midlife, and the crisis was that we had nothing to show for it—nothing but a second mortgage, an upside-down car payment, and about $20,000 in credit-card debt.

We had done just about everything we could do wrong financially. I even opened a business on credit cards!

We had tried just about every "get out of debt quick" fix there was on the market. We had even ordered several of the late-night info-mercial "extra income" kits! Talk about paying a stupid tax! Then it happened. My brother-in-law, of all people, turned us on to Dave Ramsey's plan. I was absolutely blown away. I understood what Dave was saying! Pam was in a state of shock and, understandably, disbelief. We began to work the plan. I could even help others do it.

We had our $1,000 emergency fund in just three weeks! It was the first time we'd had $1,000 in the bank for more than ten minutes. Pam knew I meant business this time, and that was good for both of us. First, that I meant business, and second, that she could really believe me. Seven weeks in, we were sailing. We had paid off two credit cards, cut up all the rest, and we used focused intensity. Everything was going great.

Then Pam's company "downsized." We lost two-thirds of our income in one day. OUCH! We didn't panic. Thank goodness for the emergency fund. We stuck with the plan and encouraged each other. Pam and I both did odd jobs to create extra income. We worked the plan, and the plan worked. We're not debt-free yet, but we walk in financial peace. We really do. Our relationship is better than ever. We moved halfway across the country so I could start a new job, and our income is back to where it was when Pam lost her job. In about three or four months (I'm on commission), we'll be debt-free!

> *Ken (age 43)*
> *and Pam (age 44) Munday*
> *Associate Pastor;*
> *Account Executive*

This emergency fund is not for buying things or for vacation; it is for emergencies only. No cheating. Do you know who Murphy is? Murphy is that guy with all those negative laws like "If it can go wrong, it will." For years I have worked with people who felt that Murphy was a member of their families. They have spent so much time with trouble that they think trouble is a first cousin. Interestingly enough, when we have had a Total Money Makeover, Murphy leaves. A Total Money Makeover is no guarantee of a trouble-free life, but my observation has been that trouble, Murphy, is not as welcome in homes that have an emergency fund. Saving money for emergencies is Murphy repellent! Being broke all the time seems to attract ol' Murphy to set up residence.

Most of America uses credit cards to catch all of life's "emergencies." Some of these so-called emergencies are events like Christmas. Christmas is not an emergency; it doesn't sneak up on you. Christmas is always in December, they don't move it, and therefore it is not an emergency. Your car will need repairs, and your kids will outgrow their clothes. These are not emergencies; they are items that belong in your budget. If you don't budget for them, they will feel like emergencies. Americans use the credit cards to cover actual emergencies too. Things discussed earlier, like job layoffs, are real emergencies and are the reason for an emergency fund. A leather couch on sale is not an emergency.

> Christmas is not an emergency.

Whether the emergency is real or just poor planning, the cycle of dependence on credit cards has to be broken. A well-planned budget for anticipated things and an emergency fund for the truly unexpected can end dependence on credit cards.

The first major Baby Step to your Total Money Makeover is to begin the emergency fund. A small start is to save $1,000 in cash *fast!* If you have a household income under $20,000 per year, use $500 for your beginner fund. Those who earn more than $20,000 should get together $1,000 fast! Stop everything and focus.

Since I hate debt so much, people often ask why we don't start with the debt. I used to do that when I first started teaching and counseling, but I discovered that people would stop their whole Total Money Makeover because of an emergency—they felt guilty that they had to stop debt-reducing to survive. It's like stopping your whole fitness program because you get a sore knee from a fall when running; you'll find any excuse will do. The alternator on the car would go out, and that $300 repair ruined the whole plan because the purchase had to go on a credit card since there was no emergency fund. If you use debt after swearing off it, you lose the momentum to keep going. It is like eating seven pounds of ice cream on Friday after losing two pounds that week. You feel sick, like a failure.

So start with a little fund to catch the little things before beginning to dump the debt. It is like drinking a light protein shake to fortify your body so you can work out, which enables you to lose weight. The beginner fund will keep life's little Murphys from turning into new debt while you work off the old debt. If a real emergency happens, you have to handle it with your emergency fund. No more borrowing! You have to break the cycle.

Twist and wring out the budget, work extra hours, sell something, or have a garage sale, but quickly get your $1,000. Most of you should hit this step in less than a month. If it looks as though it is going to take longer, do something radical. Deliver pizzas, work part-time, or sell something else. Get crazy. You are way too close to the edge of falling over a major money cliff here. Remember if the Joneses (all the broke people) think you are cool, you are heading the wrong way. If they think you are crazy, you are probably on track.

> ## Myths vs. Truth
>
> **Myth:** The debit card has more risk than a credit card.
>
> **Truth:** Nope.

Hide It

When you get the $1,000, hide it. You can't keep the money handy, because it will get spent. If your $1,000 from Baby Step One is in the underwear drawer, the pizza man will get it. No, the pizza man isn't in your underwear drawer, but you will impulse-buy something if the money is easily accessible. You can put it in the bank savings account, but it cannot become overdraft protection. Don't attach the savings account to your checking to protect you from overdrafting, because then your emergency fund will get spent on impulse. I have had to learn to protect myself from me. We are not putting the money in the bank to earn money, but rather to make it hard to get. Since $1,000 at 4 percent earns only $40 per year, you aren't getting rich here, just finding a safe place to park money.

Get creative. Maria, who attended one of our classes, went to her local Wal-Mart and bought a cheap 8" x 10" frame. She framed ten $100 bills in a stack. In the space within the frame she wrote, "In case of emergency, break glass." Then she hung the emergency fund on the wall behind coats in a closet. She knew the average burglar wouldn't look there, and it would be too much trouble for her to get it out of the closet and out of the frame, so she wouldn't use it unless there was an emergency. Whether you use a simple savings account or a frame in the coat closet, get your $1,000 quickly.

Keep It Liquid

This is a small step, so take it quickly! Don't let this small first step last for months! What if you already have more than $1,000? Wow, that was easy, wasn't it? If you already have the $1,000 in anything other than retirement plans, get it out. If it is in a Certificate of Deposit with penalties, take the penalty for early withdrawal and get it out. If it is in mutual funds, get it out. If it is in savings bonds, get it out. If it is in checking, get it out. If it is in stocks or bonds, get it out. Your emergency fund, limited to $1,000 in liquid, available cash, is all that is acceptable. If you have tried to get fancy with the emergency fund, you are likely to borrow to keep from "cashing it (the cool investment) out." Details will come later in The Total Money Makeover about what to do with your fully funded emergency fund.

All money you have above and beyond the $1,000 in anything except retirement plans will be used in the next step anyway, so get ready. You won't have this money to fall back on if the alternator on your car goes out.

SHOCKING STATS

49% of Americans could cover less than one month's expenses if they lost their income.

What if you are at Baby Step Two in the next chapter, and you use $300 from your emergency fund to fix the alternator? If this happens, stop Step Two and return to Step One until the full $1,000 is replenished. Once your beginner emergency fund is funded again, you can return to Step Two. Otherwise, you will gradually do away with this small buffer and be back to old habits of borrowing to cover real emergencies.

I know some of you think this step is very simplistic. For some this is an instantaneous step, and for others this is the first time they have ever had enough control over their money to save it. For some readers, this is an easy step. For others, this is the step that will be the spiritual and emotional basis for the entire Total Money Makeover.

Lilly was such a case. A single mom with two kids, she has been divorced for eight years; struggle has been a way of life for some time. Lilly had survival debt, not stupid spoiled-brat debt. She had been ripped off with a superhigh-interest car loan, check-advance debt, and lots of credit-card debt. She had a take-home pay of only $1,200 per month with two baby birds to feed, along with a host of greedy rip-off lenders. Saving seemed like such a fairy tale to her that she had long ago lost hope of ever being able to save money. When I met her she had already begun her Total Money Makeover. After hearing me teach the Baby Steps at a live event, weeks later she dropped by a book signing to give me an unsolicited report.

As she moved through the book line, I looked up and saw a huge grin. She asked if she could give me a big hug to say thanks. How could I turn that down? As I looked at her, tears began to run down her cheeks as she gleefully told of fighting through a budget, her first ever. She told me of years of struggle. The she laughed, and everyone in line (now fully engaged) cheered when she said she now has $500 in cash saved. This is the first $500 in her adult life that is earmarked for her emergency fund. This is the first time she has had money between her and Murphy. Her friend Amy, who was with Lilly that day, told me that Lilly is a different person already. Amy said, "Even her face has changed, now that she has peace." Don't be confused; it wasn't $500 that did all that. What caused Lilly's liberation was her newfound hope. She has hope that she never had before. She has hope because she has a sense of power and control over money. Money has been an enemy her whole life, and now that she has tamed it, money is going to be Lilly's new lifelong companion.

How about you? Now is the time to decide. Is this theory, or is it real? Am I a simpleton kook, or have I found something that works? Keep reading, and we will decide together.

7

The Debt Snowball:
Lose Weight Fast, Really

Your Total Money Makeover is dependent upon using your most powerful tools. I believe with everything within me that your most powerful wealth-building tool is your income. Ideas, strategies, goals, vision, focus, and even creative thinking are vastly important, but until you get control and full use of your income to build wealth, you will not build and keep wealth. Some of you might inherit money or win a jackpot, but that is dumb luck, not a proven plan to financial fitness. To build wealth, YOU will have to regain control of your income.

Identify the Enemy

The bottom line is that it is easy to become wealthy if you don't have any payments. You may get sick of hearing it, but the key to winning any battle is to identify the enemy. The reason I am so passionate about your getting rid of debt is that I have seen how many people make huge strides toward being a millionaire in the short time after they get rid of their payments. If you didn't have a car payment, a student loan, credit cards out your ears, medical debt, or even a mortgage, you could become wealthy very quickly. I know that may seem like a faraway place for some of you. You might feel like a 350-pounder looking at Mr. Universe, shaking your head thinking it will never happen for you. Let me assure you, I have walked with many 350-pounders into financial fitness, so stay with me.

The key to winning any battle is to identify the enemy.

The math is revealing. The typical American with a $40,000 annual income would normally have an $850 house payment and a $350 car payment, with an additional $180 payment on the second car. Then there is a $165 student loan payment; and the average credit-card debt is about $12,000, making those monthly payments around $185 per month. Also, this typical household will have other miscellaneous debt on things like furniture, stereos, or personal loans on which they pay an additional $120. All these payments total $1,850 per month. If this family were to invest that instead of sending it to the creditors, they would be cash mutual-fund millionaires in just fifteen years! (After fifteen years, it gets really exciting. They'll have $2 million in five more years, $3 million in three more years, $4 million in two and a half more years, and $5 million in two more years. So they will have $5 million after twenty-eight years.) Keep in mind, this is with an average income, which means many of you make more than this! If you are thinking that you don't have that many payments so your math won't work, you missed the point. If you make $40,000 and have fewer payments, you have a head start, since you already have more control of your income than most people.

With a take-home pay of $2,850, could you invest $1,850 if you had no payments? All you have to pay for are utilities, food, clothes, insurance, and other miscellaneous expenses. That would be tight, but doable. If you do that for just fifteen years, you will have a pinnacle experience. I will explain that later.

Many of you reading this are convinced that you could become wealthy if you could get out of debt. The problem now is that you are feeling more and more trapped by the debt. I have great news! I have a foolproof, but very difficult, method for getting out of debt. Most people won't do it because they are average, but not you. You have already figured out that if you will live like no one else, later you can live like no one else. You are sick and tired of being sick and tired, so you are willing to pay the price for greatness. This is the toughest of all the Baby Steps to your Total Money Makeover. It is so hard, but it is so worth it. This step requires the most effort, the most sacrifice, and is where all your broke friends and relatives will make fun of you (or join you). This step requires you to shave your head and drink the Kool-Aid. Just kidding, but not by much.

> "Great spirits have always found violent opposition from mediocre minds."

Your focused intensity has to go off the scale. Remember the Albert Einstein quote from earlier in the book? "Great spirits have always found violent opposition from mediocre minds."

If you really believe that wealth building will no longer be a dream but a reality if you have no payments, you should be willing to do bizarre and sacrificial things to have no payments. Time to pay off the DEBT!

Baby Step Two:
Start the Debt Snowball

The way we pay off the debt is called the Debt Snowball. The forms are on the following pages, as well as with the budget forms in the back of the book, and it is part of the Financial Peace budgeting software. The Debt Snowball process is simple to understand but will require truckloads of effort. Remember what my pastor said: "It isn't complicated, but it is difficult." We have discussed that personal finance is 80 percent behavior and 20 percent head knowledge. The Debt Snowball is designed the way it is because we are more concerned with modifying behavior than correct mathematics. (You'll see

THE DEBT SNOWBALL

List your debts in order with the smallest payoff or balance first. Do not be concerned with interest rates or terms unless two debts have similar payoffs, then list the higher interest rate debt first. Paying the little debts off first gives you quick feedback, and you are more likely to stay with the plan.

Redo this sheet each time you pay off a debt, so you can see how close you are getting to freedom. Keep the old sheets to wallpaper the bathroom in your new debt-free house. The "New Payment" is found by adding all the payments on the debts listed above that item to the payment you are working on, so you have compounding payments that will get you out of debt very quickly. "Payments Remaining" is the number of payments remaining when you get down the snowball to that item. "Cumulative Payments" is the total payments needed, including the snowball, to pay off that item. In other words, this is your running total for "Payments Remaining."

COUNTDOWN TO FREEDOM!!

Date:_____

Item	Total Payoff	Minimum Payment	New Payment	Payments Remaining	Cumulative Payments
_____	_____	_____	_____	_____	_____
_____	_____	_____	_____	_____	_____
_____	_____	_____	_____	_____	_____
_____	_____	_____	_____	_____	_____
_____	_____	_____	_____	_____	_____
_____	_____	_____	_____	_____	_____
_____	_____	_____	_____	_____	_____
_____	_____	_____	_____	_____	_____
_____	_____	_____	_____	_____	_____
_____	_____	_____	_____	_____	_____

THE DEBT SNOWBALL

Item	Total Payoff	Minimum Payment	New Payment	Payments Remaining	Cumulative Payments
————	————	————	————	————	————
————	————	————	————	————	————
————	————	————	————	————	————
————	————	————	————	————	————
————	————	————	————	————	————
————	————	————	————	————	————
————	————	————	————	————	————
————	————	————	————	————	————
————	————	————	————	————	————
————	————	————	————	————	————
————	————	————	————	————	————
————	————	————	————	————	————
————	————	————	————	————	————
————	————	————	————	————	————
————	————	————	————	————	————
————	————	————	————	————	————
————	————	————	————	————	————
————	————	————	————	————	————
————	————	————	————	————	————
————	————	————	————	————	————

what I mean shortly.) Being a certified nerd, I always used to start with making the math work. I have learned that the math does need to work, but sometimes motivation is more important than math. This is one of those times.

The Debt Snowball method requires you to list all your debts in order of smallest payoff balance to largest. List all your debts except your home; we will get to it in another step. List *all* of your debts—even loans from Mom and Dad or medical debts that have zero interest. I don't care if there is interest or not. I don't care if some have 24 percent interest and others 4 percent. List the debts smallest to largest! If you were so fabulous with math, you wouldn't have debt, so try this my way. The only time to pay off a larger debt sooner than a smaller one is some kind of big-time emergency such as owing the IRS and having them come after you, or in situations where there will be a foreclosure if you don't pay it off. Otherwise, don't argue about it; just list the debts smallest to largest.

> **Dum Math & Stupid Tax**
>
> **The Eternal Car Payment**
> Most people carry a car note for their entire lives, paying about $378 a month. That same amount invested from age 25 to retirement would, on average, amount to more than $4 million by age 65. You do the math!

The reason we list smallest to largest is to have some quick wins. This is the "behavior modification over math" part I referred to earlier. Face it, if you go on a diet and lose weight the first week, you will stay on that diet. If you go on a diet and gain weight or go six weeks with no visible progress, you will quit. When training salespeople, I try to get them a sale or two quickly because that fires them up. When you start the Debt Snowball and in the first few days pay off a couple of little debts, trust me, it lights your fire. I don't care if you have a master's degree in psychology; you need quick wins to get fired up. And getting fired up is superimportant.

Credit Card History

CARD NAME	NUMBER	ADDRESS	PHONE #	DATE CLOSED	WRITTEN CONFIRMATION REQUESTED	WRITTEN CONFIRMATION RECEIVED
Mastercard	5555 5555 5555 5555	1111 Credit Boulevard, New York, NY	201-758-2222	8/14/2001	7/14/2001	8/28/2001

My wife, Jeri, and I came from very poorly managed marriages, both financially and emotionally. Tuning in to The Dave Ramsey Show *was the best thing we could have done. We made out a monthly spending plan, better known as a "budget." My wife called the show and cut up our remaining four credit cards live on the air. We paid them off by the end of the year.*

We are currently on Baby Step Two in The Total Money Makeover *plan, the Debt Snowball. We have our home, one signature loan, and our car left to pay on. The car will be paid for in another six months, finally giving us the freedom to be done with car payments, which is a feeling we never thought we would have. Not including our home, we have about $38,000 left in debt, but in the last year we have paid off and/or sold about $35,000 worth of stuff. It's a very wonderful feeling to have done that and to be able to see the light at the end of the tunnel. We no longer receive any phones calls at home from creditors, and that is a form of freedom in itself. Our lives are a lot less stressful. We live within or below our means, and we're very happy and content now.*

We have a goal of having everything, including the home, paid for in about three to four years, at which time we will start looking for a bigger home for our family. In addition to changing our financial lives, The Total Money Makeover's *motivation encouraged us to change our physical life. My wife and I began a food budget about a year ago, and since that time we have lost a combined total of approximately 165 pounds! We can't put into words the difference we feel in our lives both financially and physically. I don't think we would ever have been able to do that if we had not*

started The Total Money Makeover plan. We will always be thank-
ful for Dave Ramsey's help and motivation. The Debt Snowball
works!

> *Kevin (age 34)*
> *and Jeri (age 24) Stuart*
> *Assistant Service Manager;*
> *Stay-at-Home Mom/*
> *Receptionist*

One lady took her Debt Snowball form to the local copy shop and had it enlarged to supersize. She then put her huge Debt Snowball on the refrigerator. Every time she paid off another debt, she drew a big red line through that debt now gone forever. She told me that every time she walked through the kitchen and looked at that refrigerator door, she would yell, "Oh, yeah, we are getting out of debt!" If that sounds corny to you, you are still not getting it. This lady has a Ph.D. She is not a dumb person. She is so sophisticated and intelligent that she got it. She under-stood that her Total Money Makeover was about a change in behavior, and that behavioral change is best enhanced by some quick (although small) wins.

When you pay off a nagging $52 medical bill or that $122 cell phone bill from eight months ago, your life is not changed that much mathe-matically *yet*. You have, however, begun a process that works, and you have seen it work, and you will keep doing it because you will be fired up about the fact that it works.

After you list the debts smallest to largest, pay the minimum payment to stay current on all the debts except the smallest. Every dollar you can find from anywhere in your budget goes toward the smallest debt until it is paid. Once the smallest is paid, the payment from that debt, plus any extra "found" money, is added to the next smallest debt. (Trust me, once you get going, you will find money.) Then, when debt number two is paid off, you take the money that you used to pay on number one and number two and you pay it, plus any found money, on number three. When three is paid, you attack four, and so on. Keep paying minimums on all the debts except the smallest until it is paid. Every time you pay one off, the amount you pay on the next one down increases. All the money from old debts and all the money you can find anywhere goes on the smallest until it is gone. Attack! Every time the Snowball rolls over, it picks up more snow and gets larger, until by the time you get to the bottom, you have an avalanche.

Most people get to the bottom of the list and find that now they can pay well over $1,000 per month on a car loan or a student loan. At that point, it won't take long to bust out and be debt-free except for the house. That is Baby Step Two: Use the Debt Snowball to become debt-free except for your home.

About eighteen months ago, I became seriously convicted about our debt. I knew there was no easy fix, and I knew it would take a while to get out. I prayed daily, and I searched high and low for solutions. Then one day I heard The Dave Ramsey Show *on the radio. Dave talked to people about having a Total Money Makeover—getting out of debt, no quick fix, no schemes, no magic button, nothing but hard work, intense focus, and what he called "gazelle intensity."*

Caller after caller sounded just like us, some worse, some better, but all about the same. When I heard Dave talk about Proverbs 22:7,

"The borrower is servant to the lender," I about ran off the road. We got intensely focused on our debt and started the Debt Snowball mentioned in The Total Money Makeover. We cleaned out our storage building, closets, and my office, and we started selling stuff through yard sales and consignment stores. We were about $35,000 in debt, but we were getting out of it now!

We are still on Baby Step Two, but our marriage is one hundred times stronger. We relate about money better, and things are great. One night not long after we started the Debt Snowball, we were in a local Kroger store, and the couple in front of us obviously had troubles. Their credit cards were maxed out, and the store would not accept their check. I hung my head in shame because we didn't have the money to help them out. For the first time, we can see light at the end of the tunnel, and it isn't an oncoming train!

Since that wonderful day of deciding to do The Total Money Makeover plan, we have paid off about $13,000 in debt. Our plan is to be debt-free except for the house in two years max. The Debt Snowball works! You get a new high every time you pay off a loan!

David (age 28)
and Chantelle (age 27) Rose
Insurance Claims Appraiser;
Stay-at-Home Mom

The Elements of Making It Work

When I first started teaching this more than fifteen years ago, I didn't understand what all the elements of success were or all the clarifications that would be needed. The major elements of making the Debt Snowball work are using a budget, getting current before you start, smallest-to-largest pay-off (no cheating), sacrifice, and focused intensity. Total, sold-out, focused intensity is possibly the most important. This means saying to yourself and meaning it, "To the exclusion of virtually everything else, I'm getting out of debt!" If you take an old-fashioned magnifying glass outside and set it near some crumpled newspapers, nothing will happen. If you point the sun's rays through the magnifying glass but move it around or wiggle it, nothing will happen. If you hold really still and focus the sun's rays totally on that crumpled newspaper, things begin to happen. Focused intensity will cause you to smell something burning, and soon you will see an actual fire.

If you think this Debt Snowball stuff is cute and you might sort of give it a try, it won't work. Total, sold-out, focused intensity is required to win. Aiming at the goal and nothing else is the only way to win. You have to know where you are going, and by definition know where you aren't going, or you will never get there. I fly a lot, and I never get on a plane and think to myself, *I wonder where this plane is heading?* I know where I want to go, and if I'm heading to New York, I stay off the plane heading to Detroit. When I get off the plane, I don't catch the first cab I see and say, "Why don't we just drive around a while because I don't have a plan." I tell them the hotel and street where I want to go. I then ask how long that will take and what the fare will be. My point is that we don't wander aimlessly around in any other parts of our lives, but we seem to think that will work with money. You can't get ready, fire, and *then* aim with money, and you can't try to do six things at the same time. You are trying to get out of debt. Period. You will have to focus with great intensity to do it.

> "To the exclusion of virtually everything else, I'm getting out of debt!"

Proverbs 6:1 and 5 (loosely Dave-paraphrased) says, "If you have signed surety, my son, [surety is Bible talk for debt] . . . deliver yourself like the bird from the hand of the fowler and the gazelle from the hand of the hunter." I remember reading that Bible verse in my daily Bible study one day and thinking what a cute little animal metaphor it was for getting out of debt. Then one day later that week I was surfing channels and hit the Discovery Channel. I noticed they were filming gazelles. The gazelles were peacefully gazelling around. Of course, you know the Discovery Channel wasn't there just for the gazelles. The next camera shot was of Mr. Cheetah sneaking up in the bushes looking for lunch in all the right places. Suddenly, one of the gazelles got a whiff of Mr. Cheetah and became very aware of his plan. The other gazelles noticed the alarm and soon also were on edge. They couldn't yet see the cheetah, so out of fear of running at him, they froze until he played his cards.

Realizing he had been discovered, Mr. Cheetah decided to give it his best shot and leaped from the bushes. The gazelles all yelled, "Cheetah!" Well, not really, but they did run like crazy in fourteen different directions. The Discovery Channel that day reminded viewers that the cheetah is the fastest mammal on dry land; he can go from zero to forty-five miles per hour in four leaps. The show also proved that because the gazelle will outmaneuver the cheetah instead of outrunning him, the cheetah will tire quickly. As a matter of fact, the cheetah only gets his gazelle burger for lunch in one out of nineteen chases. The gazelle's primary hunter is the fastest mammal on dry ground, yet the gazelle wins almost every time. Likewise, the way out of debt is to outmaneuver the enemy and *run for your life.*

> The way out of debt is to outmaneuver the enemy and *run for your life.*

Around our office, the counselors can predict who will make it out of debt based on how "gazelle intense" they are. If they are looking at a red line on the refrigerator door and yelling, they have a really good shot. However, if they are looking for a get-rich-quick scheme or some intellectual theory instead of sacrifice, hard work, and total focus, we give them a really low gazelle rating and a low probability of becoming debt-free.

The first thing I want to say is, WOW, what a year! I heard about Dave Ramsey for the first time last year. I told my wife about the radio show, and we soon became fans.

A month later we started Dave's Total Money Makeover plan. We worked on our budget and listed how much debt we had. We owed $21,700 on two cars and two credit cards. That doesn't even include our home. Together we realized that it was time to do something. As Dave would say, we went to attack mode with "gazelle intensity." The two credit cards and one vehicle were quickly paid off, leaving about $14,000 on our van. We sold stuff, had yard sales, ate at home, took our lunch to work, etc. The budget really helped. It made us think about what we would buy when we have cash in our hand.

In one of the Financial Peace University *lessons, Dave talks about being in a financial position where you can laugh at your employer if you get laid off and ask him how much the severance is. Well, it happened to me. They tapped me on the shoulder and walked me to the conference room. While walking down the hall, I was upset, but only for a minute. My mind flashed back through the year and all the things that we had done financially. I suddenly had a peace come over me and realized that God had this planned out all along and prepared us. I got a job three weeks later with better pay and better hours, and we paid off the van with my severance check. We are DEBT-FREE except for our home!*

The things that used to hurt us like car tags, Christmas, and filling up the propane tank in the winter don't get us anymore. We put the cash aside each month, and those once-a-year things aren't a struggle.

Looking at what we've accomplished, the best thing is having our budget. We would never have achieved the Debt Snowball without "gazelle intensity"! I want to thank Dave for this wonderful life-changing plan and would recommend it to everyone.

Harlon (age 33)
and Lisa (age 34) Tyree
Electronics Technician;
Program Control Analyst

An obvious step to working the Debt Snowball is to stop borrowing. Otherwise, you will just be changing the names of the creditors on your debt list. So you must draw a line in the sand and say, "I will never borrow again." As soon as you make that statement, there will be a test. Trust me. Your transmission will go out. Your kid will need braces. It is almost as if God wants to see if you are really gazelle-intense. At this point, you are ready for a plasectomy—plastic surgery to cut up your credit cards. A permanent change in your view of debt is your only chance. No matter what happens, you have to pursue the opportunity or solve the challenge without debt. It has to stop. If you think you can get out of debt without huge resolve to stop borrowing, you are wrong. You can't get out of a hole by digging out the bottom.

How to Get the Snowball Rolling

Sometimes your Debt Snowball won't roll. When some people do their budget, there is barely enough to make all the minimum payments and nothing extra to pay on the smallest. There is no push to get the Snowball rolling. Let me offer another image to help you better understand this problem and the solution. My great-great grandfather ran a timber operation in the hills of Kentucky and West Virginia. In that bygone era, after cutting the timber they would put the logs into the river to float them downstream to the sawmill. The logs would build up at a bend in the river, and a traffic jam of wood occurred. This would continue as long as the jammed-up area stopped the progress of the other logs. Sometimes the loggers could break the jam loose by pushing the logs. Other times they would have to get radical before a real mess occurred.

Dave Rants . . .

Remember, just because one of you is keeping the checkbook, this does not mean that this person makes all the financial decisions.

When it got bad, they would break the logjam by throwing dynamite into the middle of the logs that were blocking the progress. As you can imagine, this created a dramatic effect. When the dynamite blew, logs and pieces of logs would fly into the air. After working so hard to cut the trees, some of them were a total loss. They had to blow up some of the timber to get the rest of the crop to market. That's the sacrifice the situation required. Sometimes that is what you have to do with the stopped-up budget. You have to dynamite it. You have to get radical to get the money flowing again.

One way to do that is to sell something. You could sell lots of little stuff at a garage sale, sell a seldom-used item on the Internet, or sell a big precious item through the classifieds. Get gazelle-intense and sell so much stuff that the kids are afraid they are next. Sell things that make your broke friends question your sanity. If your budget is stopped-up and your Debt Snowball won't roll on its own, you are going to have to get radical.

Watching heroes across the nation get out of debt with gazelle intensity, believe me, I have seen them sell things. One lady sold 350 goldfish from her pond for a dollar apiece. Men have sold their Harleys, boats, knife collections, or baseball cards. Ladies have sold precious things like nonfamily antiques (keep the heirlooms because you can't get them back) or a personal car they thought was necessary to life on the planet.

I don't recommend selling your home unless you have payments above 45 percent of your monthly take-home pay. Usually, the home isn't the problem. I do recommend that most people sell the car with the most debt on it. A good rule of thumb on items (except the house) is this: If you can't be debt-free on it (not counting the home) in eighteen to twenty months, sell it. If you have a car or a boat that you can't pay off in eighteen to twenty months, sell it. It is just a car; dynamite the logjam! I used to love my car too, but I found keeping that huge debt

It is just a car; dynamite the logjam!

while trying to get out of debt was like running a race wearing ankle weights. Get a Total Money Makeover, so later you can drive anything you want and pay cash for it. When it comes to that debt-ridden item, you may have to make the decision to live like no one else, but remember, later you will be living, or driving, like no one else.

My husband, Scott, and I had been married for twenty years, and although we had a great marriage, financial security was not one of our benefits! We both climbed the success ladder and had a very good income, yet we still lived paycheck to paycheck and had accumulated debt totaling $120,000. Scott was not anxious to follow The Total Money Makeover plan, because he knew that we were going to be faced with a decision about changing our lifestyle. When we decided to go for it, we had decreased our personal debt by over $15,000 and cut up eleven credit cards in just thirteen weeks!

We were working with a strict budget but had not implemented the Debt Snowball at that time. Scott and I knew that we needed to step up the pace because the Lord was calling us to get out of debt and go into full-time ministry. We had accumulated a lot over the years, so we started to hold yard sales. This included the sale of our 33' Trojan Express Cruiser, our 23' camper trailer, our 1966 red Thunderbird convertible, our Kia Sportage, and a lot of other toys accumulated over the years. God was at work throughout this process because Scott's pride and joy was his T-Bird, and to give that up was giving up a lot.

Since we started The Total Money Makeover, we have paid off over $65,000 of our $120,000 debt, and continue with our Debt Snowball (which is now in place) to be completely out of debt in less than two years. We have no house mortgage, so once the remaining $55,000 is paid off (which includes one last credit card, a bank loan, and two cars), we will be totally DEBT-FREE!

Our children have been very supportive throughout this process and have joined us in developing a different lifestyle. We have made a commitment as a family to become debt-free, and it takes the support of every member to do so. We have truly changed our family tree and have done so before it was too late to reach our children. I would like to thank Dave Ramsey for his message of hope. Our marriage and family are much stronger because of the changes we have put into place.

Donna MacPherson (age 42)
Nursing Home Administrator

The number of people I talk to about this who will not throw dynamite into their logjam to get the money flowing makes me sad. They can see that the logs will never get to market, they will never have wealth, but they just can't stand the thought of blowing up a few of them so the rest will get down the river. Translation: "I love my stupid car more than the idea of becoming wealthy enough to give cars away." Don't make that mistake.

There is another method of breaking your logjam that the lumberjacks didn't have available to them. More water would have pushed the logs around that corner, too, if they could have flooded the river. I may be stretching this metaphor, but more income will also break up your logjam, will push the Snowball. If your budget is too tight to get the Debt Snowball rolling, you need to do something to increase income. Selling debt-ridden items lowers the outgo, and selling other items temporarily increases our income. Likewise, working extra hours can increase income in order to increase the speed of debt repayment.

I don't like the idea of working one hundred hours per week, but

SHOCKING STATS

60% don't pay off their credit cards every month.

sometimes extreme situations require extreme solutions. Temporarily, just for a manageable period of time, the extra job or overtime may be your solution. I met Randy while doing a book signing in a major city. Randy was two months from being debt-free. He is twenty-six years old and has paid off $78,000 in debt in twenty-one months. He sold a car and works ten hours a day, seven days a week. Randy is not a doctor or lawyer; he is a plumber. Some lawyers would argue that plumbers make more than they do, and in some cases they might be right. Randy's one-man plumbing company has prospered. He had already worked that morning before coming with his wife and little girl to the bookstore. His wife smiled as she looked at her husband with deep respect and told me she hadn't seen him much this last year, but it was going to be worth it soon. Can you imagine the pressure that young marriage must have been under with $78,000 in debt? Now they are almost free.

Randy got radical. He used income to bust the logjam. He promised me he was going to slow down as soon as the debt was paid so he could spend time with his wife and little girl. Now they will be able to go places as a family and do things their debt would never have allowed them to do.

I picked up a pizza last night, and as the guy behind the counter started walking toward his car with a stack of pizzas to be delivered, he saw me and stopped. Smiling, he said, "Hey, Dave, I'm here because of you. Only three more months, and I'm debt-free!" This was not some seventeen-year-old teenager; this was a dad, a thirty-five-year-old guy who wants to be free. There is a young single guy that works on my team. He is gazelle-intense about becoming debt-free. He works here until 5:30 every day, and he smiles as he leaves to work for UPS for another four or five hours virtually every night.

> ## Myths vs. Truth
>
> **Myth:** I'll just file bankruptcy and start over; it seems so easy.
>
> **Truth:** Bankruptcy is a gut-wrenching, life-changing event that causes lifelong damage.

Why are these guys all smiling? They work hard and unbelievable extra hours, so why would they smile? They smile because they have caught the vision, the vision of living like no one else so later they can live like no one else.

What About Saving for Retirement While the Snowball's Rolling?

Matt asked me on the radio show about another subject people have trouble with on Baby Step Two. Matt wanted to know if he should stop his 401k contributions to get his Debt Snowball moving. He really didn't want to stop contributing, especially the first 3 percent because his company matches that 100 percent. I am a math nerd, and I know the 100 percent match is sweet, but I have seen something more powerful—focused intensity. If you are going to be gazelle-intense and do everything in your power to become debt-free very quickly, then stop your retirement plan contributions, even if your company matches them. The power of focus and quick wins is more important in the long term to your Total Money Makeover than is the match. This is only for people who have already pulled out all the stops and are ready for "anything goes" to become debt-free quickly.

If you are radically gazelle-intense, the speed of your debt freedom will enable you to return to that 401k with the match in just a matter of months. Imagine how much you'll be able to contribute without payments. The average person who throws the dynamite and is gazelle-intense will be debt-free except for his or her home in eighteen months. Some take longer and others less, depending on debt, income, and savings at the time they start their Total Money Makeover. If for some reason you are stuck in an extremely deep hole, you may want to continue doing some retirement saving. An extremely deep hole is NOT defined by your unwillingness to apply yourself. An extremely deep hole is not Phil's situation.

Phil makes $120,000 per year with $70,000 of debt, $32,000 of which is on one car. Sell the car and amputate the lifestyle, Phil. Phil should be debt-free in nine months, no excuses, and no prisoners. An extremely deep hole is Tammy's situation. Tammy has $74,000 in student loans with another $15,000 in credit-card debt. Tammy is a single mom with three children and has an income of $24,000 per year. It is going to take Tammy a few years to work her Debt Snowball. She will figure a way through it, but her situation is one of the very rare exceptions; she should keep contributing to the 401k with the match.

When You Have to Dip In to the Emergency Fund

Penny's air conditioner went out in the dead of summer. The repairs were $650, which she took from her emergency fund. "Thank goodness that $1,000 was there," she said with a sigh. Now what does she do? The Debt Snowball, or stop and go back to Baby Step One (save $1,000)? Penny needs to put the Debt Snowball temporarily on hold. She will continue to make minimum payments and go back to the first step until she gets back up to $1,000 in her emergency fund. If she doesn't, soon she will have nothing in savings, and when the alternator on the car goes out, she will reopen some credit-card account. The same applies to you. If you use the emergency fund, return to Baby Step One until you have re-funded your beginner emergency fund, then move right back to your Debt Snowball, Baby Step Two.

Second Mortgages, Business Debt, and Rental Property Mortgages

Because of debt consolidation loans and other mistakes, many people have a home equity loan or some kind of large second mortgage. What should be done with this loan? Is it put in the Debt Snowball, or just called a mort-gage and not dealt with at this step? It will be paid off; it is just a matter of at which step. Generally speaking, if your second mortgage is more than 50 percent of your gross annual income, you should not put it in the Debt Snowball. We will get to it later. If you make $40,000 per year and have a $15,000 second mortgage, you should put it in the Debt Snowball. Let's just take care of it now. But if you have a $35,000 second and make $40,000, you will get to it in another step. By the way, you should consider refinancing your first and second mortgages together if you can lower both interest rates. Then put the total on a fifteen-year mortgage, or the remain-ing years of your current first mortgage, whichever is less (e.g., if you have twelve years remaining on your first mortgage at 9 percent, refinance the first and second mortgages together into a new first at 6 percent over twelve years or less).

Many small-business owners have debt and want to know how to handle that debt in the Debt Snowball. Most small-business debt is per-sonally guaranteed, which means it is really personal debt. If you have a small-business loan of $15,000 at the bank or have borrowed on your credit cards for business, this is personal debt. Treat small-business debt like any other kind of debt. List it with all your other debts, smallest to largest, in the Debt Snowball. If your business debt is larger than half your gross annual income or half your home mortgage, hold the payoff on that size debt until later. Smaller and medium-sized debts are what we want to pay off at this step.

The only other larger debt to delay are mortgages on rental properties. Stop buying more rental property, but hold that debt until later. After your home mortgage is paid off in a later Baby Step, you should Snowball your rental mortgages. List the rental debts smallest to largest, and concentrate all your focus on the smallest until paid. Then work your way through the rest. If you own several, or even just one, rental property, you should consider selling some or all to get the money to pay off the ones you keep or pay off other debt listed in the Debt Snowball. Having $40,000 in credit-card debt and a rental with $40,000 equity doesn't make sense. You wouldn't borrow $40,000 on credit cards to buy a rental, I hope. So why would you keep the situation described here, which has the same effect?

Other than the home mortgage, larger second mortgages, business loans, and rental mortgages are the only things that aren't paid off in Baby Step Two (Start the Debt Snowball). With gazelle intensity, great focus, extreme sacrifice, selling things, and working extra, we clear all debt. Again, if you are fired up, normally this will happen within eighteen to twenty months. Some will get out of debt sooner, and some will get out in a slightly longer period of time. If your Snowball is scheduled to run longer, never fear, it may not take as long as the math seems to indicate. Many people find a way to shorten the time with sheer intensity, and God tends to pour blessings on people going in a direction He wants them to go. It is as if you are walking or running at a fast pace, and a moving sidewalk suddenly appears below you to carry you faster than your own effort would.

> God tends to pour blessings on people going in a direction He wants them to go.

The Debt Snowball is very possibly the most important step in your Total Money Makeover for two reasons. One, you free up your most powerful wealth-building tool, your income, during this step. Two, you take on the entire American culture by declaring war on debt. By paying off your debt, you make a statement about your stance on the issue of debt. By paying off your debt, you show that The Total Money Makeover of your heart has occurred, paving the way for a Total Money Makeover of your actual wealth.

8

Finish the Emergency Fund: Kick Murphy Out

Close your eyes and think about what it will be like when you reach this Baby Step. Most gazelle-intense participants in a Total Money Makeover will arrive at the beginning of Baby Step Three in around eighteen to twenty months. When you reach this step, you have $1,000 cash and no debt except your home mortgage. You have pushed with such focused intensity that the ball is now rolling, and you have momentum on your side. Again, close your eyes and breathe in. Think about what it will feel like when you are debt-free except for the house and have $1,000 cash. Did I see you smiling?

You are beginning to see the power of being in control of your largest wealth-building tool, your income. Now that you don't have any payments, except the house, Baby Step Three should come quickly.

Baby Step Three: Finish the Emergency Fund

A fully funded emergency fund covers three to six months of expenses. What would it take for you to live three to six months if you lost your income? Financial Planners and Financial Counselors like myself have used this rule of thumb for years, and it has served my Total Money Makeover

133

participants well. You start the emergency fund with $1,000, but a fully funded emergency fund will usually range from $5,000 to $25,000. The typical family that can make it on $3,000 per month might have a $10,000 emergency fund as a minimum. What would it feel like to have no payments but the house, and $10,000 in savings for when it rains?

> It will rain; you need an umbrella.

Remember what we said about emergencies a couple of chapters back? It *will* rain; you need an umbrella. Don't forget, *Money* magazine says 78 percent of us will have a major unexpected event within the next ten years. When the big stuff happens, like the job layoff or the blown car engine, you can't depend on credit cards. If you use debt to cover emergencies, you have backtracked again. A well-designed Total Money Makeover will walk you out of debt forever. A strong foundation in your financial house includes the big savings account, which will be used just for emergencies.

When my husband and I started The Total Money Makeover, we had an annual household income of $73,000. The only problem was that we had $28,000 in debt. Our debt was the usual— credit cards, student loans, second mortgage, and two kids in private schools costing $6,000 per year, mostly paid through our credit cards!

Soon after we started the plan, my husband was laid off from his job as Vice President of Finance at a small company. Even though we had only started the plan three weeks before, we already had the emergency fund in place. IT WAS THE ONLY WAY WE MADE IT!

With the inspiration of The Total Money Makeover plan, we managed to do odd jobs here and there until we had funded our *emergency fund. We are currently down to $24,500 in debt and have a plan in place that will have everything but the house paid off within a year!*

My husband just started a new job with better pay than before, but we know now to live below our means and continue to budget EVERY dollar. Before, we just thought, We have plenty of money, so let's spend it. *Not anymore!*

We've been out of debt a couple of times before but kept falling back into it because we didn't have the wisdom, knowledge, and discipline to stay out of debt. Dave Ramsey has been like a personal counselor and accountability partner to us.

Glenn (age 39)
and Stephanie (age 40) Jackson
Chief Financial Officer;
Professional Musician

I'm going to bang on this drum again because it is vital if your makeover is going to be permanent. The worst time to borrow is when times are bad. If there is a recession and you lose your job (read, "no income"), you don't want to have a bunch of debt. In a recent Gallup poll, 78 percent of Americans said they would borrow on a credit card if a rainy day came, and it wouldn't be difficult. I agree it wouldn't be difficult because credit cards are issued to dogs and dead people every year, but that doesn't mean it would be smart. What would be difficult is to make the payments and even pay off the debt if you don't get that new replacement job. A poll in *Parenting* magazine said 49 percent of Americans could cover less than one month's expenses if they lost their income. Half of this culture has virtually no buffer between them and life. Here comes Murphy! Remember how we discussed that problems seem to be (and I believe actually are) less frequent when you have your fully funded emergency fund? Don't forget that the emergency fund actually acts as Murphy repellent.

So what is an emergency anyway? An emergency is something you had no way of knowing was coming, something that has a major impact on you and your family if you don't cover it. Emergencies include paying the deductible on medical, homeowner's, or car insurance after an accident, a job loss or cutback, medical bills resulting from an accident or unforeseen medical problem, or a blown transmission or engine in a car that you need to function.

All of these are emergencies. Something on sale that you "need" is not an emergency. Fixing the boat, unless you live on it, is not an emergency. "I want to start a business" is not an emergency. "I want to buy a car or a leather couch or go to Cancún" is not an emergency. Prom dresses and college tuition are not emergencies. Beware not to rationalize the use of your emergency fund for something that you should save for and purchase. On the other hand, don't make payments on medical bills after an accident while your emergency fund sits there fully funded. If you've gone to the trouble of creating an emergency fund, make sure you are crystal clear on what is and is not an emergency.

> Beware not to rationalize the use of your emergency fund for something that you should save for and purchase.

Before using the emergency fund, back up from the situation and calm down. Sharon and I would never use the emergency fund without first discussing it and being in agreement. We also would never use the emergency fund without sleeping on the decision and praying about it. Our agreement, our prayer, and our cooling-off period all help us determine if this decision is a rationalization, a reaction, or a real emergency.

The Emergency Fund Must Be Easy to Access

Keep your emergency fund in something that is liquid. *Liquid* is a money term that means easy to get to with no penalties. If you would hesitate to use the fund because of the penalties you'll incur to get to it, you have it in the wrong place. I use growth-stock mutual funds for long-term investing, but I would never put my emergency fund there. If my car engine blew, I would be tempted to borrow to fix it rather than cash in my mutual fund because the market is down (we always want to wait on it to go back up). That means I have the emergency fund in the wrong place. Mutual funds are good long-term investments, but because of market fluctuations you are likely to have an emergency when the market is down—another invitation to Murphy. So keep your emergency fund liquid!

> ### SHOCKING STATS
>
> 78% of Americans said they would borrow on a credit card if a rainy day came.

For the same reason, don't use Certificates of Deposit for your emergency fund because typically you will be charged a penalty for making an early withdrawal. The exception to this is if you can get some kind of "quick-release" CD that allows one withdrawal during the committed period without penalty. That quick release makes the money available to you without penalty and would make that CD a good emergency fund. Understand, you don't want to "invest" the emergency fund, just have it someplace safe and easy to get to.

If you already have emergency-fund money someplace it shouldn't be, use your head if a true emergency hits you. Christine, a sixty-nine-year-old grandmother, told me she borrowed to fix her transmission because she didn't want to pay a penalty to cash out her CD. The loan was her "wise" banker's suggestion, and Christine trusted her banker. The only problem is, even with the penalty, Christine would have been better off to cash out her CD. The repair cost was $3,000. Her CD earned 5 percent, and the penalty for cashing it out early was half the interest. So her banker loaned her $3,000 at 9 percent interest so she wouldn't lose 2.5 percent in penalties. Doesn't sound too wise to me. Honestly, it doesn't sound too ethical to me either. Words are powerful; none of us want to be "penalized." When emotions took over, Christine trusted instead of thinking and made a bad decision.

I suggest a Money Market account with no penalties and full check-writing privileges for your emergency fund. We have a large emergency fund for our household in a mutual-fund company Money Market account. Wherever you get your mutual funds, look at the Web site to find Money Market accounts that pay interest equal to one-year CDs. I haven't found bank Money Market accounts to be competitive. The FDIC does not insure the mutual-fund Money Market accounts, but I keep mine

> ## Dum Math & Stupid Tax
>
> ### Shocking Numbers on Winning the Lottery
>
> Of people making less than $35,000 per year, 40 percent said the best way for them to have $500,000 at retirement age is to win the Lotto. Your chances of winning the lottery are about 1 in 15 million. You're 10 times more likely to be struck by lightning.

there anyway because I've never known one to fail. Keep in mind that the interest earned is not the main thing. The main thing is that the money is available to cover emergencies. Your wealth building is not going to happen in this account; that will come later, in other places. This account is more like insurance against rainy days than investing.

Sometimes, even after I've explained all this, people still ask about savings bonds, bonds, or other "low-risk" investments. They are missing the point. Again, this emergency fund is not for wealth building. You will get other kinds of return on investment from this account, but the purpose of this money is not to make you rich. The mission statement for the emergency fund is to protect you against storms, give you peace of mind, and keep the next problem from becoming debt.

How Big?

So how much money should be in your emergency fund? We said it should be enough to cover three to six months of expenses, but should you go with three months or six months? If you think about the purpose of this fund, it will help you determine what is right for you. The purpose of the fund is to absorb risk, so the more risky your situation, the greater the emergency fund you should have. For example, if you earn straight commission or are self-employed, you should use the six-months rule. If you are single or you are a one-income married household, you should use the six-months rule because a job loss in your situation is a 100 percent cut in household income. If your job situation is unstable or there are chronic medical problems in the family, you, too, should lean toward the six-months rule.

I discovered The Total Money Makeover a little over two years ago. At the time, I had over $53,000 in debt. Today my debt equals $0!

My savings two years ago consisted of a rollover IRA of around $15,000, and a few thousand dollars in a regular savings account. Savings next year will break into the six figures! It took a while for The Total Money Makeover message to "sink in," but I found myself making small changes the more I listened to The Dave Ramsey Show.

When I took the new job, I had to do the usual "new job" mantra by buying a new car, etc. At the time I had a $20,000 student loan, credit-card debt of around $6,000, and a miscellaneous loan for *around $4,000. The $6,000 in credit-card debt was "revolving," meaning I would pay it down to a point, then recharge items back to a $5,000, $6,000, or $7,000 balance. This process has occurred since college. In fact, the last time I can remember being debt-free was when I first started college thirteen years ago.*

But that's all changed now! In addition to paying off all my debt, I have been able to save a large amount of money on a regular basis. My goal is to pay cash for a house when I decide to leave the nomad traveling life of consulting. The incremental changes that I made after discovering The Total Money Makeover started with cutting up, and getting off, the credit-card merry-go-round. This was a monumental move and a major relief.

The next change after my savings started increasing was to pay the credit-card balance and the miscellaneous loan, and to build up my emergency fund. Next, after a period of months, the student loan that I had for ten years was paid off, and recently I wrote a check for $6,000 to pay off my car!

I am totally DEBT-FREE and have six months' worth of income in my emergency fund!

> *Ford W. Chambliss (age 37)*
> *Software Consultant*

If you have a "steady, secure" job where you have been with that company or government agency for fifteen years and everyone is healthy, you could lean toward the three-month rule. A real estate agent should have a six-month fund, and a healthy postal worker who has been in her job for years and plans to stay might keep a three-month fund. Customize your emergency fund to your situation and to how your spouse deals with the feeling of risk. Many times men and ladies deal with this subject differently. This fund is for actual protection and for peace of mind, so the spouse who wants this fund to be higher wins.

We use three to six months of expenses instead of three to six months of income because the fund is to cover expenses, not replace income. If you become ill or lose a job, you need to keep the lights on and food on the table until things turn around, but you might stop investing, and you'll definitely stop spending budgeted "blow money" until the rain clears. Of course, when you are just starting your Total Money Makeover, your expenses might equal your income. Later when you are debt-free, you have all the right insurance in place, and you have large investments, you can survive on much less than your income.

Use All Available Cash

In Baby Step Two, I instructed you to use all nonretirement savings and investments to pay down your debt. Clean everything out and become debt-free except for the house. Use all savings and investments that don't have a penalty for withdrawal like retirement plans. If you used savings that you had in Baby Step Two (Start the Debt Snowball), you cleaned out even the emergency fund down to Baby Step One (Save $1,000). Now is the time to rebuild your emergency fund by replacing any money you may have used to pay debt. Many times I've met someone who, for example, had $6,000 in savings at the bank making 2 percent interest, and $11,000 in credit-card debt. The very thought of using $5,000 of that savings to pay the credit cards partially off is very hard. That $6,000 emergency fund is your security blanket, and fear rises up deep inside when someone like me mentions that you should use that money to Snowball your debt. You are right to feel that fear and to question whether you should spend the $5,000 to pay down the debt. You should use that money ONLY if you and your whole family are into a Total Money Makeover. Gazelle intensity, budgeting, selling ankle-weight cars, and overall total commitment to the plan are the only way using that savings makes sense.

You Need All Parties Completely On Board

Sherry called our radio show saying that her husband wanted to use $9,000 of their $10,000 emergency fund on Baby Step Two, but he wanted to keep his $21,000 truck debt—with a household income of $43,000. Sherry was mad at me for suggesting something so absurd. Of course, I didn't make that suggestion. I think it would be a bad move for them to use $9,000 in this situation. The reason I'm against using the savings as suggested is that hubby isn't on board. He wants to do part of the plan and keep his stupid truck. There are two reasons not to use the emergency fund in Sherry's case. First, Hubby has not had a Total Money Makeover in his heart, and they will never make it out of debt under any strategy until he does. Second, do the math: On a $43,000 income, they will be in debt and have only a supersmall emergency fund for years if they keep the truck. This would be like my wife saying she wants me to lose weight and then baking homemade chocolate-chip cookies every night. She would be saying one thing and doing another.

Dave Rants ...

To make more money, you have to plan to make more money. Some people's problem is income, not spending.

I don't suggest you clean out your savings if everyone isn't having a Total Money Makeover. I also don't suggest you clean out your savings if you are planning to be in Baby Step Two (Start the Debt Snowball) for five years. However, few of you will be in Step Two very long if you go gazelle-intense and follow this plan to the letter. If your family is exposed to the elements, with only $1,000 standing between you and life for eighteen to twenty months, that is fine. In that case, you should use your savings to become debt-free or accelerate the Snowball.

I know even if everyone is on board, gazelle-intense, and there is a plan, my suggestion still scares some of you. Good. Don't you think one of the things that make the gazelle intense is fear? For a short period of time, while you work your Debt Snowball and rebuild your emergency fund in Step Three, use that fear as a motivator to stay focused and keep everyone else moving.

The good news in Sherry's story is that her hubby heard her on the radio with me, and a lightbulb came on. He sold "his" truck, she used "her" savings, and in fourteen months they were debt-free; in eighteen months, they were debt-free with a fully funded emergency fund. Sherry sent an e-mail to me about an amusing part of their journey. She said after they were debt-free and rebuilding her precious emergency fund with the same gazelle intensity they used to pay the debt, one of their teens asked them to buy a computer. Before Sherry could say no, her hubby grabbed the teen in a loving headlock and started yelling, in jest, that there would be no purchases in that house until the emergency fund was done. This made Sherry smile because it told her that not only was the emergency fund coming back soon, but that her husband had gotten the message of how important that fund was to her. She was willing to have a Total Money Makeover, but only if it was Total—for both of them.

Gender and Emergencies

The sexes do view the emergency fund differently. In general, men are more task oriented, and ladies are more security-based. Guys like to know what you "do," so some of us don't understand the idea of money just sitting there causing security. Most ladies I meet smile when we start talking about having $10,000 between them and the rain. Many of them say the emergency fund and life insurance are the best parts of their family's Total Money Makeover.

Guys, let's talk. God wired ladies better on this subject than He did us. Their nature causes them to gravitate toward the emergency fund. Somewhere down inside the typical lady is a "security gland," and when financial stress enters the scene, that gland will spasm. This spasmodic gland will affect your wife in ways you can't always predict. A spasmodic security gland can affect her emotions, her concentration, and even her love life. Apparently, the security gland is attached to her face. Can you see the financial stress on her face? Believe me, guys, one of the best investments you will ever make is in an emergency fund. A fully funded emergency fund and a husband in the midst of a Total Money Makeover will relax the security gland and make your life much better. My friend Jeff Allen, comedian, does a whole routine on "Happy Wife, Happy Life." The bottom line is that even if you don't "get" the emergency fund, get one.

I already told you that Sharon and I lost everything, went broke, crashed, and were at the bottom, so you can imagine that this subject is a little sensitive at my house. Our financial crash was totally my doing: It was my real estate business screwup that Sharon watched before she took the ride with me. One of the wounds in our relationship is this issue of security. Her emotions can revisit the fear of looking at a brand-new baby and a toddler and not knowing how we were going to keep the heat on. That is a sensitive place in her psyche, and with good reason. We don't even use the emergency fund for emergencies. Part of the salve on that wound is that our emergency fund has an emergency fund. If I even walk near the drawer where the emergency fund Money Market checkbook is kept, Sharon's security gland can tighten up.

Being the highly trained investment mogul that I am, I could certainly find places to put that money where it would earn more. Or would it? Remember, personal finance is personal. I have come to realize that Sharon's peace of mind bought with the oversized emergency fund is a great return on investment. Guys, this can be a wonderful gift to your wife.

An Emergency Fund Can Turn Crises into Inconveniences

As you budget over the years and your Total Money Makeover completely changes your money habits, you will use the emergency fund less and less. We haven't touched our emergency fund in over ten years. When we first started, everything was an emergency. But as you crawl off the bottom, and The Total Money Makeover begins to take effect, you have fewer things you can't cover in your monthly budget. At the start, though, you'll be like we were—everything will be an emergency. To show you what I mean, consider two different stories of people at two different places in the Baby Steps.

Kim is twenty-three, single, on her own, and at a job making $27,000 per year. She started her Total Money Makeover last week. She was behind on credit cards, not on a budget, and barely making her rent because her spending was out of control. She let her car insurance drop because she "couldn't afford it." Last week, she did her first budget and two days later was in a car wreck. Since it wasn't bad, the damage to the other guy's car was only about $550. As Kim looked at me through panicked tears, that $550 might as well have been $55,000. She hadn't even started Baby Step One. She was trying to get current, and now she had one more hurdle to clear before she even started. This was a huge emergency.

Seven years ago, George and Sally were in the same place. They were broke with new babies, and George's career was sputtering. George and Sally fought and scraped through a Total Money Makeover. Today they are debt-free, even their $85,000 home. They have a $12,000 emergency fund, retirement in Roth IRAs, and even the kids' college is funded. George has grown personally, his career has blossomed, and he now makes $75,000 per year while Sally stays home with the kids. Last week, a piece of trash flew out of the back of George's pickup and hit a car behind him on the interstate. The damage was about $550.

I think you can see that George and Sally will probably adjust one month's budget and pay the repairs while Kim will deal with her wreck for months. The point is that as you get in better shape, it takes a lot more to rock your world. When the accidents occurred, George's heart rate didn't even change, but Kim needed a Valium sandwich to calm down.

Those true stories illustrate the fact that as you progress through your Total Money Makeover, the definition of an emergency that is worthy to be covered by the emergency fund changes. As you have better health insurance, disability insurance, more room in your budget, and better cars, you will have fewer things that qualify as emergency-fund emergencies.

What used to be a huge, life-altering event will become a mere inconvenience. When you are debt-free and aggressively investing to become wealthy, taking a few months off from investing will put a new engine in a car. When I say the emergency fund is Murphy repellent, that is only partially correct. The reality is that Murphy doesn't visit as much, but when he does we hardly notice his presence. When Sharon and I were broke, our heating-and-air system quit, and the repair cost $580. It was a huge, hairy deal. Last month I had a new $570 water heater installed because the old one started leaking, and I hardly noticed. I wonder if the stress relief that your Total Money Makeover provides will allow you to live longer?

> What used to be a huge, life-altering event will become a mere inconvenience.

Let Me Be Perfectly Clear

There are some Baby Step Three clarifications. Joe asked recently if he should stop his Snowball—Step Two—to get his emergency fund finished. Joe and his wife have twins due in six months. Brad's plant is closing in four months, and he will lose his job. Mike got a huge severance check of $25,000 last week when his company downsized him. Should these people work on debt or finish the emergency fund? All three should temporarily stop Snowballing and concentrate on the emergency fund because we can see distant storm clouds that are real. Once the storm passes, they can resume the plan as before.

Resuming the plan for Joe means that once the babies are born healthy, are home, and everyone is fine, Joe will take the emergency fund back down to $1,000 by using the rest of the savings to pay the Debt Snowball. Resuming for Brad would mean that once he finds his new job, he'll do the same. Mike should hold his instant emergency fund of $25,000 until he is reemployed. The sooner he can get a job, the more that severance is going to look like a bonus and have a huge impact on the Debt Snowball.

Sometimes people think they don't need an emergency fund because their income is guaranteed. Richard is retired military and receives over $2,000 per month, which he could live on if he lost his job. He didn't think he needed an emergency fund because he thought all emergencies were job-related. Then he had a car wreck the same month he was laid off. His $2,000 kept coming, but now he faced car debt. Even if your income is guaranteed, you still might need to help a sick relative, replace your heating system in the middle of winter, or get a new transmission. Large, out-of-budget emergencies that aren't job-related do come up and will require the emergency fund.

If You Don't Own a Home

I keep saying that you are debt-free except for the house at this point and saving to finish the emergency fund. What if you don't have a home yet? When do you save for the down payment? I am going to talk as many of you as possible into the 100 percent down plan, but I know some of you will take the fifteen-year fixed-rate mortgage that I said earlier is okay.

I love real estate, but do not buy a home until you finish this step. A home is a blessing, but if you move into home ownership with debt and no emergency fund, Murphy will set up residence in the spare bedroom.

I believe in the financial and emotional advantages of home ownership, but I have known many stressed-out young couples who rushed to buy something before they were ready.

Saving for a down payment or cash purchase of a home should

> ## Myths vs. Truth
>
> **Myth:** That collector was so helpful; he really likes me.
>
> **Truth:** Collectors are not your friends.

occur after becoming debt-free in Step Two and after finishing the emergency fund in Step Three. That makes saving for a down payment Baby Step Three (b). You should save for the home if you have the itch before moving on to the next step. Many people are worried about getting a home, but please let it be a blessing rather than a curse. It will be a curse if you buy something while you are still broke. There are all sorts of folks who are eager to "work with you" so you can make it happen sooner, but the definition of "Creative Financing" is "Too Broke to Buy a House."

Next Stop: Serious Wealth Building

Well, you have made it. You are now debt-free except for the home mortgage, and you have three to six months of expenses saved. Getting to the end of this step if you are gazelle-intense takes the typical family twenty-four to thirty months. Two or two and a half years from the time you start your Total Money Makeover, you can sit at the kitchen table with no payments, other than for the house, and with around $10,000 in a Money Market account. Close your eyes one more time and let your emotions and your spirit visit that place. Wow, I know I see you smiling now.

My parents were divorced when I was nine years old; therefore, my mother had to work to take care of my three sisters and me. I helped get my sisters up in the mornings and off to school. When my mom and dad were married, I thought we were doing okay until our cars and furniture were repossessed. At the age of sixteen, I decided I wanted to know my father again and moved to his state. When I was eighteen years old, my father decided to move away, but I had found the woman of my dreams and wasn't moving for any reason. My father was killed at the age of thirty-nine after getting in an argument with his brother over money; my uncle shot him.

At the age of eighteen, I was totally on my own. I worked two jobs at a time, if not three. After dating my high-school sweetheart for three years, we were married. We thought we'd live the lifestyle her parents had lived, and we ran credit cards up and got car payments. You know the drill.

After ten years of living in debt, I started listening to The Dave Ramsey Show *and told my wife, "I think we can have a better life than what we have now." So we embarked on a fifteen-month journey to get out of debt. In that period, we paid off over $25,000 in credit cards, put a new roof on the house, put two new transmissions on our two cars, and bought many other small items, all on a household income of under $70,000.*

Almost a year after being debt-free except for our home, I've got my fully funded emergency fund, and I'm now a Dave Ramsey Certified Financial Counselor, out there helping others change their family tree.

As a side note, this past year I became the Business Administrator at my church, and after five months our church is now DEBT-FREE! We hope to build a new church in the fall.

Russell Sisk (age 32)
Customer Representative

I am very demanding and very passionate about following these principles and steps precisely because I have seen people like the ones on these pages win doing The Total Money Makeover. I have heard every excuse, every whining reason, and every rationalization as to why you are different and you have a better way, but trust me, you don't. The good thing about principles is that they make life easy. I have heard it said that when someone bases his life on principle, 99 percent of his decisions are already made.

> The good thing about principles is that they make life easy.

Once we have covered these basic steps and laid a foundation, the time has come to build some wealth. Remember, that is why we started a Total Money Makeover. We wanted not just to be out of debt, but to become wealthy enough to give, retire with dignity, leave an inheritance, and have some expensive fun. Stay tuned for some big fun.

9

Maximize Retirement Investing: Be Financially Healthy for Life

I have a friend in his forties who has a bodybuilder physique. He is lean with well-defined muscle groups, but he is not some wild health nut. He watches what he eats and works out a couple of times a week. I have another friend in his thirties who diets fanatically, runs every day, lifts weights three times a week, but is still forty pounds overweight. The second guy started his health journey a couple of years ago and is losing weight and getting in shape. The first muscle man maintains what he worked hard years ago to get, but he isn't working nearly as hard today.

The Total Money Makeover is the same way. Gazelle intensity is required to get to the wealth steps, but simple maintenance will keep your money muscles maintained. Keep in mind that my muscle-man friend never eats three plates of food at a sitting. He is still aware he can lose his fitness, but he can look good and feel good with a lot less effort, assuming he remembers the principles that got him his great body in the first place.

> Simple maintenance will keep your money muscles maintained.

Gazelle intensity has allowed you to lose one hundred pounds of debt and get your cardio emergency fund ready. That foundation will allow you to become financially fit by toning your muscles. You have attacked your debt; it is gone.

151

With the extra money after eliminating your debt, you attacked your emergency fund; it is funded. You are now at a crucial time. What do you do with the extra money that you poured into the emergency fund and debt payoffs? This is not the time to give yourself a raise! You have a plan, and you are winning. Keep it up! You are two quarters into a four-quarter game. It is time to begin with the end in mind! It is time to invest.

What Retirement *Isn't*

Investing for retirement in the context of a Total Money Makeover doesn't necessarily mean investing to quit your job. If you hate your career path, change it. You should do something with your life that lights your fire and lets you use your gifts. Retirement in America has come to mean "Save enough money so I can quit the job I hate." That is a bad life plan.

Harold Fisher is one hundred years old. He works five days a week at the architectural firm he founded. Mr. Fisher doesn't work because he needs money, not by a long shot. He works because he finds joy in what he does. He is a designer of churches. His favorite saying is, "People who retire early, die early." "If I retired, what would I do?" he asks. Harold Fisher is financially secure and able to do what he wants, and that defines *retirement* The Total Money Makeover way.

> If you hate your career path, change it.

When I speak of retirement, I think of security. Security means choices. (That's why I think retirement means work is an option.) You can choose to write a book, to design churches, or to spend time with your grandkids. You need to reach the point where your money works harder than you do. A Total Money Makeover retirement plan means investing with the goal of security. You already possess the ability to quit your job, and if you don't like your work, you should consider doing that. If not today, develop a five-year game plan for transitioning into what God designed you to do; however, don't wait till you're sixty-five to do what you love.

That said, the money part does matter. You want to reach your golden years with financial dignity. That will happen only with a plan. *USA Today* reported recently that 56 percent of Americans do not systematically prepare for retirement age by investing. Not only have we not done anything about retiring with dignity, we have lost hope that it is even possible. Consumer Federation of America found that of people making less than $35,000 per year, 40 percent said the best way for them to have $500,000 at retirement age is to win the Lotto. Wow! These people need a Total Money Makeover in a big way! If you want another peek at the warped view of reality we have, consider that *Wealth Builder* magazine's poll found 80 percent of Americans believe their standard of living will go *up* at retirement. Talk about living in a fantasy!

My wife, Becki, and I lived the first thirteen years of our married life with credit cards, car notes, and an occasional home equity loan. We were "normal" Americans. We went to Hawaii and committed one of the better acts of stupidity and bought a time-share with a credit card. We finally "woke up" shortly after we got back from that trip. We found ourselves with $35,000 in debts, not including the home mortgage, which still had a balance close to $180,000. We didn't have an emergency fund to speak of either. Had I lost my job, we would have had to sell the house almost immediately in order to survive. Plus, we were saving NOTHING for retirement! This was NOT a fun way to live.

I had heard about The Total Money Makeover through a friend. I decided we needed to follow the plan and pull ourselves out of a scary mess. It took a little over two years to pay off the $35,000, but we did it! We now have $11,000 in an emergency fund and, most important, we are putting 15 percent of our income into 401ks and Roth IRAs so we are prepared for retirement!

Bottom line? We are now much more comfortable and have found some of that peace that had been missing in our lives. Our thanks to Dave Ramsey's Total Money Makeover for kicking us into gear and providing the game plan to get us here! Now we will retire with financial dignity!

Steve Fogle (age 45)
Construction Controller

The reality is much colder. *USA Today* reports that out of one hundred people age sixty-five, ninety-seven of them can't write a check for $600, fifty-four are still working, and three are financially secure. Bankruptcies among those sixty-five and older have gone up 164 percent in the last eight years. Getting older is going to happen! You must invest now if you want to spend your golden years in dignity. Investing with the long-term goal of security is not a theory to ponder every few years; it is a necessity you must act on now. You must actually fill out the paperwork for your mutual fund. You must actually put money in that thing. According to these statistics, the level of denial the average person has on this subject is alarming.

Baby Step Four:
Invest 15 Percent of Your Income in Retirement

Those of you concerned about retirement are relieved we have finally gotten to this step. Those who have been living in denial are wondering what all the fuss is about. Baby Step Four is time to get really serious about your wealth building. Remember, when you reach this step you don't have any payments but a house payment, and you have three to six months' worth of expenses in savings, which is thousands of dollars. With only one payment, it should be easy to invest heavily. Even with a below-average income, you can ensure your golden years will have dignity. Before this step, you have ceased or have never started investing, and now you have to really pour on the coals.

Gazelle intensity in the previous steps has allowed you to be able to focus on growing a sizable nest egg. The tens of thousands of people we have met have helped me develop the 15 percent rule. The rule is simple: Invest 15 percent of before-tax gross income annually toward retirement. Why not more? You need some of your income left to do the next two steps, college saving and paying off your home early. Why not less? Some people want to invest less or none so they can get a child through school or pay off the home superfast. I don't recommend that because those kids' college degrees won't feed you at retirement. I don't recommend paying off the house first because I have counseled too many seventy-five-year-olds with a paid-for house and no money. They end up selling the family home or mortgaging it to eat. Bad plan. You need some retirement investing at this stage before saving for college and the mortgage payoff. Plus, by getting started now, the magic of compound interest will work for you.

When calculating your 15 percent, don't include company matches in your plan. Invest 15 percent of your gross income. If your company matches some or part of your contribution, you can consider it gravy.

> ### Dum Math & Stupid Tax
>
> **A Doubly-Wide Financial Loss**
>
> If you buy a $25,000 double-wide home, in five years you will owe $22,000 on a trailer worth $8,000. Financially, it's like living in your new car. I'm not above living in a mobile home (I've lived in worse), but they are lousy places to put money.

Remember, this is a rule of thumb, so if you cheat down to 12 percent or up to 17 percent, that is not a huge problem, but understand the dangers of straying far from 15 percent. If you underinvest, you will one day be buying that classic cookbook, *72 Ways to Prepare Alpo and Love It*. If you overinvest, you will keep your home mortgage too long, which will hold back the wealth-building power of your Total Money Makeover.

By the same token, do not use your potential Social Security benefits in

> It is your job to take care of you and yours.

your calculations. I don't count on an inept government for my dignity at retirement, and you shouldn't either. A recent survey said more people under age thirty believe in flying saucers than believe they will receive a dime from Social Insecurity. I tend to agree. I'm not taking a political position (although I'm not above it), but the mathematics of that system spell doom. I'm not Chicken Little predicting the sky is falling; entire books have been written on the Social Security mess. Understand, it is your job to take care of you and yours, so part of your Total Money Makeover is to invest now to make that happen. If Social Security isn't there when you retire, you'll be glad you listened to my advice. If by some miracle Social Security is there when you retire, that will mean I was wrong. In that case, you'll have some extra money to give away. I'm sure you'll forgive me for that.

Your Tool Is Mutual Funds

Now that you have reached this step, you need to learn about mutual funds. The stock market has averaged just below 12 percent return on investment throughout its history. Growth-stock mutual funds are what I recommend investing in for the long term. Growth-stock mutual funds are lousy short-term investments because they go up and down in value, but they are excellent long-term investments when leaving the money longer than five years. Ibbotson Research says that 97 percent of the five-year periods and 100 percent of the ten-year periods in the stock market's history have made money. *The Total Money Makeover* is not an investment textbook, so if you need more detailed information, check out our class, Financial Peace University, or my first book, *Financial Peace*. My personal retirement funds and my kids' college are invested the way I teach in the *The Total Money Makeover*.

Here's a *Reader's Digest* version of my approach. I select mutual funds that have had a good track record of winning for more than five years, preferably for more than ten years. I don't look at their one-year or three-year track records because I think long term. I spread my retirement investing evenly across four types of funds. Growth and Income funds get 25 percent of my investment. (They are sometimes called Large Cap or Blue Chip funds.) Growth funds get 25 percent of my investment. (They are sometimes called Mid Cap or Equity funds; an S&P Index fund would also qualify.) International funds get 25 percent of my investment. (They are sometimes called Foreign or Overseas funds.) Aggressive Growth funds get the last 25 percent of my investment. (They are sometimes called Small Cap or Emerging Market funds.) For a full discussion of what mutual funds are and why I use this mix, go to daveramsey.com and visit MyTMMO.

Dave Rants . . .

The reason you are afraid of investing is because you do not know what you are getting into. Learn about investments.

The invested 15 percent of your income should take advantage of all the matching and tax advantages available to you. Again, our purpose here is not to teach the detailed differences in every retirement plan out there (see my other materials for that), but let me give you some guidelines on where to invest first. Always start where you have a match. When your company will give you free money, take it. If your 401k matches the first 3 percent, the 3 percent you put in will be the first 3 percent of your 15 percent invested. If you don't have a match, or after you have invested through the match, you should next fund Roth IRAs.

The Roth IRA will allow you to invest $3,000, $4,000, or $5,000 per year, per person, depending on which year you read this book. There are some limitations as to income and situation, but most people can invest in a Roth IRA. The Roth grows tax-FREE. If you invest $3,000 per year from age thirty-five to age sixty-five, and your mutual funds average 12 percent, you will have $873,000 tax-FREE at age sixty-five. You have invested only $90,000 (30 years x 3,000); the rest is growth, and you pay no taxes. The Roth IRA is a very important tool in virtually anyone's Total Money Makeover.

Start with any match you can get, and then fully fund Roth IRAs. Be sure the total you are putting in is 15 percent of your total household gross income. If not, go back to 401ks, 403bs, 457s, or SEPPs (for the self-employed), and invest enough so that the total invested is 15 percent of your gross annual pay.

Example:

Household Income   **$47,000**

Husband   **$27,000**

Wife   **$20,000**

Husband's **401k** matches **first 3%**.

3% of **27,000 ($810)** goes into the **401k.**

Two Roth IRAs are next, totaling **$6,000.**

The goal is **15%** of **47,000**, which is **$7,050.**

You have **$6,810** going in. So now you bump the husband's **401k** to **4%**, making the total invested **$7,080.**

What It Will Take to Retire

How much do you need to retire with dignity and security? How long will it take you to get there? See the following pages for worksheets to help you calculate some of these actual numbers. You are secure and will leave a nice inheritance when you can live off 8 percent of your nest egg per year. If you make 12 percent on your money average and inflation steals 4 percent, 8 percent is a dream number. If you make 12 percent and only pull out 8 percent, you grow your nest egg by 4 percent per year. That 4 percent keeps your nest egg, and therefore your income, ahead of inflation 'til death do you part. You get a cost-of-living raise from your nest egg every year. If you can live with dignity on $40,000, you need a nest egg of only $500,000. I would recommend that you have the largest nest egg possible because there are some really cool non-greedy things to do with it later, like giving it away.

If, when you run the calculations on the worksheet, you are afraid you won't make your goal of saving 15 percent, keep in mind that this is just Baby Step Four. Later steps will allow you to accelerate your investing while still having a life.

Would you dream with me for a moment? Dream that a twenty-seven-year-old couple with average to below-average income commit to a Total Money Makeover. They get gazelle-intense, and in three years, by age thirty, they are at Step Four. They invest 15 percent of their income in four types of growth-stock mutual funds with five- to ten-year track records. The average household income in America is $40,816 per year, according to the Census Bureau. Joe and Suzy Average would invest $6,000 (15 percent) per year or $500 per month. If you make $40,000 per year and have no payments except the house mortgage and live on a budget, can you invest $500 per month? Follow me here. If Joe and Suzy invest $500 per month with no match into Roth IRAs from age thirty to age seventy, they will have $5,882,386 tax-FREE! That is

Monthly Retirement Planning

In order to retire with some security, you must aim at something. Too many people use the READY-FIRE-AIM approach to retirement planning. Your assignment is to determine how much per month you should be saving at 12% interest in order to retire at 65 years old with what you need.

If you are saving at 12%, and inflation is at 4%, then you are moving ahead of inflation at a net of 8% per year. If you invest your nest egg at retirement at 12% and want to break even with 4% inflation, you will be living on 8% income.

Step One:
Annual Income (today) you wish to retire on: $30,000

divide by .08

(Nest egg needed) equals: $375,000

Step Two:
To achieve that nest egg, you will save at 12%, netting 8% after inflation, so we will target that nest egg using 8%.

$375,000	X	.000436 =	$163.50
Nest Egg Needed		Factor	Monthly Savings Needed

8% Factors (select the one that matches your age)

AGE	YEARS TO SAVE	FACTOR
25	40	.000286
30	35	.000436
35	30	.000671
40	25	.001051
45	20	.001698
50	15	.002890
55	10	.005466
60	5	.013610

Note: Be sure to try one or two examples if you wait 5 or 10 years to start.

Monthly Retirement Planning

In order to retire with some security, you must aim at something. Too many people use the READY-FIRE-AIM approach to retirement planning. Your assignment is to determine how much per month you should be saving at 12% interest in order to retire at 65 years old with what you need.

If you are saving at 12%, and inflation is at 4%, then you are moving ahead of inflation at a net of 8% per year. If you invest your nest egg at retirement at 12% and want to break even with 4% inflation, you will be living on 8% income.

Step One:
Annual Income (today) you wish to retire on: $_____
divide by .08

(Nest egg needed) equals: $_____

Step Two:
To achieve that nest egg, you will save at 12%, netting 8% after inflation, so we will target that nest egg using 8%.

_____ X _____ = _____
Nest Egg Needed   Factor   Monthly Savings Needed

8% Factors (select the one that matches your age)

AGE	YEARS TO SAVE	FACTOR
25	40	.000286
30	35	.000436
35	30	.000671
40	25	.001051
45	20	.001698
50	15	.002890
55	10	.005466
60	5	.013610

Note: Be sure to try one or two examples if you wait 5 or 10 years to start.

Retirement Options

The changes under the Economic Growth and Tax Relief Reconciliation Act of 2001 affect some retirement plans. The salary-reduction limits are as follows:

YEAR	401K/403B/SAR-SEP	SIMPLE	457
2001	$10,500	$6,500	$8,500
2002	$11,000	$7,000	$11,000
2003	$12,000	$8,000	$12,000
2004	$13,000	$9,000	$13,000
2005	$14,000	$10,000	$14,000
2006	$15,000	$10,000	$15,000
2007 and Following Fully Phased In	Adjusted for Inflation	Adjusted for Inflation	Adjusted for Inflation

There are also new salary-reduction <u>catch-up</u> contributions that can be made for those individuals who reach 50 years of age during the plan year.

YEAR	401K/403B/457/SAR-SEP	SIMPLE IRA
2002	$1,000	$500
2003	$2,000	$1,000
2004	$3,000	$1,500
2005	$4,000	$2,000
2006	$5,000	$2,500
2007 and Following	Adjusted for Inflation	Adjusted for Inflation

Also, the Economic Growth and Tax Relief Reconciliation Act of 2001 provides a new IRA annual contribution and catch-up limit for those 50 years old and older.

YEAR	MAXIMUM IRA CONTRIBUTION	ADDITIONAL CATCH-UP
2002-2004	$3,000	$500
2005-2007	$4,000	$500 ($1,000 in 2006-2007)
2008	$5,000	$1,000
AFTER 2008	ADJUSTED FOR INFLATION IN $500 INCREMENTS	$1,000

almost $6 million. What if I'm half wrong? What if you end up with only $3 million? What if I'm six times wrong? Sure beats the 97 out of 100 sixty-five-year-olds who can't write a check for $600!!

I would submit to you that Joe and Suzy are well below average. Why? In our example they started at the average household income in America, and in forty years of work never got a raise. They saved 15 percent of income and never increased it by one dollar. There is no excuse to retire without financial dignity in the United States today. Most of you will have well over $2 million pass through your hands in your working life-time, so do something about catching some of that money.

Gayle asked me one day if it was too late for her to start saving. Gayle wasn't twenty-seven like Joe and Suzy. She was fifty-seven years old, but with her attitude you would have thought this lady was 107. Harold Fisher has a much better outlook at age one hundred

Myths **vs.** Truth
Myth: If I do a will, I might die.
Truth: You *are* going to die—so do it with a will.

than Gayle did at age fifty-seven. Life had dealt her some blows and had knocked most of the hope out of her. A Total Money Makeover is not a magic show. You start where you are, and you do the steps. These steps work if you are twenty-seven or fifty-seven, and they don't change. Gayle might be starting the retirement investing step at sixty that Joe and Suzy start at thirty years old. Gayle is unwise to enter her sixties without an emergency fund and with credit-card debt and a car payment. She, like all of us, can't save when she has debt and no umbrella for when it rains. Would it have been better for Gayle to start when she was twenty-seven or even forty-seven? Obviously. But once she's done with the pity party, she still needs to start with Baby Step One and follow The Total Money Makeover step-by-step to put herself in the best position possible.

It is never too late to start. George Burns won his first Oscar at eighty.

Golda Meir was prime minister of Israel at seventy-one. Michelangelo painted the ceiling of the Sistine Chapel lying on his back on scaffolding at seventy-one. Colonel Sanders never fried any chicken for money until he was sixty-five, and Kentucky Fried Chicken is a household name world-wide. Albert Schweitzer was still performing surgery in Africa at eighty-nine. It is never too late to start. The past has passed. Start where you are, because that is your only option. However, a note to all of you under forty: All of us over forty are giving you a collective yell, "INVEST NOW!"

Baby Step Four is not "Get rich quick." The investing you do systematically and consistently over time will make you wealthy. If you play with this by jumping in and out, always finding something more important than investing, you are doomed to being one of those 54 out of 100 sixty-five-year-olds still working because you have to work. Systematic, consistent investing is the tortoise that beats the hare in the race. When you keep at it, the investing compounds and explodes. The following by Timothy Gallway always reminds me of this concept:

> It is never too late to start.

When we plant a rose seed in the earth, we notice it is small, but we do not criticize it as "rootless and stemless." We treat it as a seed, giving it the water and nourishment required of a seed.

When it first shoots up out of the earth, we don't condemn it as immature and underdeveloped; we do not criticize the buds for not being open when they appear. We stand in wonder at the process taking place, and give the plant the care it needs at each stage of its development.

The rose is a rose from the time it is a seed to the time it dies. Within it, at all times, it contains its whole potential. It seems to be constantly in the process of change: Yet at each state, at each moment, it is perfectly all right as it is.

A flower is not better when it blooms than when it is merely a bud; at each stage it is the same thing . . . a flower in the process of expressing its potential.

The story of the rose is about human potential and about not being defined by what you do, but rather who you are. Your Total Money Makeover and the stage your investments are in are similar. Push with gazelle intensity to bloom, but know that as long as you take the progressive steps, *you are winning*. Ultimately, we are not defined by wealth; however, your Total Money Makeover will affect your wealth, as well as your emotions, relationships, and spiritual condition. This is a "Total" process.

Our journey began three years ago, and to date we have had slightly over a $140,000 positive swing in our financial situation. We are winning! This was done by staying "focused," some hard work, spousal communication, and sacrifice. The Total Money Makeover affects all areas of your life. Let me preface our accomplishments by saying that we are normal working people. We have accomplished the following goals without selling any possessions over $2,000, and without receiving any windfalls of money or inheritances.

Here is what we've accomplished due to the plan:

- *Paid off $33,000 in credit cards*
- *Established an emergency fund of $14,000*

- *Terminated our car "fleece" and paid $19,000 cash for a two-year-old Jeep Grand Cherokee*

- *Purchased $1M in term life insurance*

- *Made $15,000 "paid in cash" upgrades to our home*

- *Contributed $50,000 and growing in our 401k and TSA!*

It has been a long four years, but we are not finished; we continue to save in our 401ks and plan to attack our mortgage!

It took some short-term sacrifices; my husband began working nights at Kroger, and I took on extra tutoring assignments at my school. It has been a long road for us, and yet we are a stronger family unit because of this. I think we are better parents and better people because of the experiences we have had. My husband and I talk about the goals we have for ourselves and for our children's future. Thank you for The Total Money Makeover information you provide, for the stories that make us shake our heads in disbelief, and for the opportunity to find financial peace.

Steve (age 38)
and Kim Llorens (age 39)
Account Executive;
Schoolteacher

After completing this step, you have no debt, except the house, around $10,000 cash for emergencies, and you are taking steps to make sure

You are going to win.

you will retire with dignity. I think I see a smile broadening. I know when Sharon and I reached this step things started to move in our lives. We started to regain the confidence that losing everything had taken from us. You are going to win. Can you feel it? Can you see it? If not, go back and read that sentence again. Better yet, write it where you'll see it every day: "I am going to win!" Your life is changing! This is fun! Now, let's take another step.

10

College Funding:
Make Sure the Kids Are Fit Too

Time to do something about the ever-famous college fund. Many of you have been wringing your hands while we walked through four Baby Steps and have not saved so much as a dime for those little cherubs. Some people in our culture have lost their minds about college education. College is important, so important that I've explained to my kids that if they don't go to college, we will hire people to do mean things to them until they go. Seriously, a solid education to begin your adult life and your career will add to the quality of both. I also attended and graduated from college; go figure.

Understand the Purpose of a College Education
Before You Fund It

I have done financial counseling for parents who I was afraid would need years of therapy if they didn't provide their children the most expensive school, free for the taking. I am sure that as we start this Baby Step we need to examine our culture's value system on the college issue. We have sold our young people so hard and so long on college that we have begun to accept some myths about college degrees. College degrees do not ensure jobs. College degrees certainly don't ensure success. College degrees do not ensure wealth. College degrees only prove that someone has successfully passed a series of tests. We all know college-educated people who are broke and unemployed. They are very disillusioned because they thought they had bought a ticket and yet were denied a seat on the train to success.

College degrees do not ensure wealth.

If you are sending your kids to college because you want them to be guaranteed a job, success, or wealth, you will be dramatically let down. In some cases, the letdown won't take long because as soon as they graduate they will move back in with you. Hear me on this: College is great, but don't expect too much from that degree. What if we were to admit that, in most cases, college can only teach knowledge? If we did, we'd see that failure and heartache are guaranteed—if we expect a college degree by itself to deliver life's treasures. Only if you mix knowledge with attitude, character, perseverance, vision, diligence, and extreme levels of work will your college degree produce for you. We have placed a dangerous responsibility on that thin little sheepskin. We have asked that it do things it cannot do.

Because we have turned a college degree into some kind of "genie in a bottle" formula to help us magically win at life, we go to amazingly stupid extremes to get one. I have been a millionaire starting with nothing two times before I was forty, and I attribute 15 percent of that to college knowledge and 0 percent to the degree. The book *Emotional Intelligence* reported a similar finding. In studying successful people, the author discovered that 15 percent of success could be attributed to training and education, while 85 percent was attributed to attitude, perseverance, diligence, and vision. If we admit out loud that education is for knowledge, which is only part of the formula to success, then we don't have to lose our minds in pursuit of the Holy Grail degree.

What about those lifelong friends your children will make in college who can "help" them when they graduate? Let me ask you: Have you made any extra money because of friendships you made in college? I'm not saying friendships don't matter, or even that college friends won't ever help you in your career; however, if the price for those kinds of friendships is major debt, it's way too high. Besides, you can build quality relationships for the future no matter where you attend school.

> ## Myths vs. Truth
>
> **Myth:** Leasing a car is what sophisticated people do. You should lease things that go down in value and take the tax advantage.
>
> **Truth:** Consumer advocates, noted experts, and a good calculator will confirm that the car lease is the most expensive way to operate a vehicle.

We need this foundation of why we want college for our kids in order to set goals for school. In other words, if you do not expect quite as much from the degree, maybe you won't break all the branches in your family tree getting the kids into someplace you frankly can't afford. Again, college is important—very important—but it is not the answer to all your kids' problems. I will be so bold as to say college isn't even a need; it is a want. It isn't a necessity; it is a luxury. This luxury is one of the first on my list, but not before retirement, not before an emergency fund, and certainly not as a reason to go into debt.

Dave's Rules for College

Do some research on the cost of attending college. Find out what your old college costs today. Find out what the big state school in your area costs. Find out what the smaller state school in your neighborhood costs. Find out what the private smaller, more intimate college costs. Compare them. In some areas of study and in a very few careers, where you graduate from will matter, but in most it won't. Pedigree means less and less in our work culture today. How can you justify going into debt $75,000 for a degree when you could have gone to a state school and paid for it out of your pocket debt-free? You can't. If you have the $75,000 extra cash or a free-ride scholarship and want to go to that private school debt-free, by all means, do it. Otherwise, reconsider.

The first rule of college (whether for you or for your children) is: Pay cash. The second rule is: If you have the cash or the scholarship, go. A couple of years ago, I met with the dean of the college of business from the university where I graduated. At that time, the average college student graduated with about $15,000 in student-loan debt after spending three of four years in an apartment, not the dorm, and eating off-campus, not on the meal plan. The average student paid $5,000 *more per year* to live and eat off-campus than to live in the dorm and eat cafeteria food. The student loans that they "had to have" or they wouldn't be able to go to college weren't for college at all. The student loans, on average, paid for an off-campus standard of living, and no debt was needed to get the degree, only to look good while getting the degree.

> Stay away from loans; make plans to avoid borrowing.

Student loans are a cancer. Once you have them, you can't get rid of them. They are like an unwelcome relative who comes to stay for a "few days" and is still in the guest room ten years later. We have spread the myth that you can't be a student without a loan. Not true! *USA Today* says that in 1992, 42 percent of students took loans, while in 2000, 64 percent of students took loans. Student loans have become normal, and normal is broke. Stay away from loans; make plans to avoid borrowing.

If you've planned your savings goals and don't have much room in the budget for college, don't panic. Knowledge is just part of the formula to success. With what you are able to save, those precious kids can probably get a good degree if they will suffer through lifestyle adjustments and get a job while in school. Work is good for them. In past generations, students lived with relatives, slept in dorms, ate cafeteria food, and endured other hardships to get a degree. They even went to schools without pedigrees to get the knowledge, which is what they were after. They also were under no illusions of the degree giving them guaranteed jobs or success.

Now, after spending pages harping on mind-set, we can set some reasonable, attainable goals for saving for college.

Baby Step Five:
Save for College

Virtually everyone thinks that saving for college is important; however, hardly anyone saves money for their kids' college education. *Money* magazine and CBS Market Watch both quote the alarming statistic that 39 percent of Americans with kids don't save a dime toward college. Four percent have saved less than $1,000, and 25 percent have saved between $1,000 and $10,000. That means 68 percent have saved nothing or close to nothing! Why are we doing so badly? Because we are in debt, have no emergency savings, no budget, and so on. We have to Baby-Step our way here in our Total Money Makeover before we have the money to save for college. If you save for college and don't have an emergency fund, you will raid the college fund to keep the home out of foreclosure when you get laid off. If you try to save for college while making payments on everything under the sun, you won't have any money to save. On the other hand, by the time you get here in the Baby Steps, you'll have a strong foundation and

> *Dum Math & Stupid Tax*
>
> **Very Interest-ing!**
>
> If your mortgage payment is $900 and the interest portion is $830, you will pay that year around $10,000 in interest. What a great tax deduction! Right? Otherwise, you'd pay $3,000 in taxes on that $10,000. But who in their right mind would choose to trade $10,000 for $3,000?

money to save. If you don't have children, or your kids are grown and gone, you will simply skip this step. For everyone else, a college fund is a necessity. And, if you do what I say, when you do start a college fund, you won't end up raiding it.

We were a two-income family, making $50,000 combined. That was pretty good in the late '80s. We were rolling along just fine, spending every dime we made. We were expecting our first child, and my wife's boss wanted her to work full-time. My company was bought out, and I was let go. So, to make it, I had the brilliant idea to borrow our way out of debt! Very quickly we were $50,000 in debt, with two car payments, and only $30,000 in salary. Needless to say, our marriage was getting stressed. We had to make a positive move.

I went into sales and doubled my income. We cut up all the credit cards (ten of them) and sent out cancellation letters. We finally figured out that debt was not the way to wealth. We sold both our one-and-a-half-year-old cars and bought a $3,000 four-year-old car for cash, one that we shared. Yes, sometimes it was a little inconvenient, but not nearly as inconvenient as having no money and a ton of bills! Two moves later, I started a new job and grossed more in my first year than we made combined early in our marriage. We were really able to start paying off the debt now!

We finally got rid of the last of the credit cards (yes, even the "pay it off" American Excess one!). We are now on Baby Step Five. We have $20,000 in savings, we're putting back college funds, and we have eleven years left on our fifteen-year mortgage. We pay cash for *vacations . . . nice vacations. Beyond all this, we really do have a lot of hope and peace, thanks to Dave Ramsey and The Total Money Makeover plan. Our marriage has grown to a new level! We will have money for our child's college! My wife actually believes that there is stability in our family and can trust that she can have what she wants. Eliminate your addictions to stuff, and you can have a changed life, too!*

Derek (age 42)
and Karen (age 42) Anderson
Senior Account Executive;
Stay-at-Home Mom

ESAs and 529s

College tuition goes up faster than regular inflation. Inflation of goods and services averages about 4 percent per year, while tuition inflation averages about 7 percent per year. When you save for college, you have to make at least 7 percent per year to keep up with the increases. Baby life insurance, like Gerber or other Whole Life for babies to save for college, is a joke, averaging less than a 2 percent return. Savings bonds won't work either (sorry, Grandma!) because they average about 5 percent. Most states now offer prepaid college tuition. We discussed that in Chapter 4 on Money Myths, but remember that when you prepay anything you simply break even with inflation on that item. If tuition goes up 7 percent a year and you prepay it, you make 7 percent on your money. That is not too bad, but keep in mind that a decent growth-stock mutual fund will average over 12 percent when invested long-term. Of course, there are worse things than prepaid tuition. *USA Today* reports that 37 percent of the few who actually save for college do so in a simple savings account yielding less than 3 percent. That won't get it done. I know, something's better than nothing. But I like another adage better in this case: If something's worth doing, it's worth doing right. Let's do Baby Step Five the right way.

I suggest funding college, or at least the first step of college, with an Educational Savings Account (ESA), funded in a growth-stock mutual fund. The Educational Savings Account, nicknamed the Education IRA, grows tax-free when used for higher education. If you invest $2,000 a year from birth to age eighteen in prepaid tuition, that would purchase about $72,000 in tuition, but through an ESA in mutual funds averaging 12 percent, you would have $126,000 tax-free. The ESA currently allows you to invest $2,000 per year, per child, if your household income is under $200,000 per year. If you start investing early, your child can go to virtually any college if you save $166.67 per month ($2,000/year). For most of you, Baby Step Five is handled if you start an ESA fully funded and your child is under eight.

If your children are older, or you have aspirations of expensive schools, graduate school, or Ph.D. programs that you pay for, you will have to save more than the ESA will allow. I would still start with the ESA if the income limits don't keep you out. Start with the ESA because you can invest it anywhere, in any fund or any mix of funds, and change it at will. It is the most flexible, and you have the most control. To do some detailed planning, check out the worksheet on the next page. This will help you calculate how much you need to save to hit your college goal.

If you want to do more than the ESA, or your income rules you out, you may want to look at a 529 plan. These are state plans, but most allow you to use the money at any institution of higher learning, which means you can save in New Hampshire's 529 plan and go to college in Kansas. There are several types of 529 plans, and you should stay away from most of them. The first type to become popular was the "life phase" plan. This type of plan allows the plan administrator to control your money and move it to more conservative investments as the child ages. These perform poorly (at about 8 percent) because they are very

Monthly College Planning

In order to have enough for college, you must aim at something. Your assignment is to determine how much per month you should be saving at 12% interest in order to have enough for college.

If we are saving at 12%, and inflation is at 4% then we are moving ahead of inflation at a net of 8% per year.

Step One:

In today's dollars how much per year the college of your choice costs: $_____

   X 4 years = $_____

(hint: $15,000 to $25,000 annually)

Step Two:

To achieve that college egg, you will save at 12%, netting 8% after inflation, so we will target that college egg using 8%.

_____ X _____ = _____

  Nest Egg Needed   Factor   Monthly Savings Needed

8% Factors (select the one that matches your child's age)

CHILD'S AGE	YEARS TO SAVE	FACTOR
0	18	.002083
2	16	.002583
4	14	.003247
6	12	.004158
8	10	.005466
10	8	.007470
12	6	.010867
14	4	.017746

Note: Be sure to try one or two examples if you wait 5 or 10 years to start.

conservative. The next type is a "fixed portfolio" plan, which sets a fixed percentage of your investment in a group of mutual funds and locks you in until you need the money. You can't move the money, so if you get into some stinky funds, you're stuck with them. This type may yield better returns, but it gives you less control—still something to take a pass on.

One of the problems with a 529 plan is that you must give up an element of control. The best 529 plans available, and my second choice to an ESA, is a "flexible" plan. This type of plan allows you to move your investment around periodically with a certain family of funds. A family of funds is a brand name of mutual fund. You could pick from virtually any mutual fund in the American Funds Group or Vanguard or Fidelity. You are stuck in one brand, but you can choose the type of fund, the amount in each, and move it around if you want. This is the only type of 529 I recommend.

Regardless of how you save for college, do it. Saving for college ensures that a legacy of debt is not passed down your family tree. Sadly, most people graduating from college right now are deeply in debt before they start. If you start early or save aggressively, your child will not be one of them.

Two car payments, one mortgage, and credit-card payments describe us before Financial Peace University. *Our total consumer debt was about $22,000. We were newlyweds and had already listened to* The Dave Ramsey Show *on the radio for about a year. By the time we started* The Total Money Makeover plan, *we had been on a budget for about nine months and had already paid off around $10,000. After being on a budget for a couple of months, we felt we had gotten a major pay raise.*

We had practiced all of Dave Ramsey's philosophies before we saw him at one of his live event speaking engagements.

We paid off another $6,000 in debt after officially starting the plan! We felt that we were in the "driver's seat" for the first time. In the spring we bought a house (fifteen-year Conventional mortgage) that is about twice as big as what we had been in. I was able to quit work and go back to school on the GI Bill since I am retired military. My wife is such a go-getter that she has doubled her salary in only five years. I will finish school next spring and have begun working part-time. I will now be able to get a great job. We were able to take a three-week paid-for vacation to Italy last May, and our emergency fund sits at $6,000.

We are doing great! We recently opened an Educational Savings Account for our grandson. With the support built into The Total Money Makeover and a little life practice, anyone can change the family tree. Help yourself to a more fulfilling and less stressful life. Start the plan ASAP!

Wes (age 49) and
Dina (age 51) Loukota
Both Programmers/Developers

Getting Creative When You Don't Have Much Time

What if you have only a couple of years and will not be able to save much because you started your Total Money Makeover later in life? First, revisit the concepts at the beginning of the chapter. Plan on your child attending somewhere that is cheaper, living on campus, and eating the cafeteria food. Knowledge is what you are after, not a pedigree. Student loans are off-limits. You must get creative and resourceful. Have your children think of companies that might be looking to hire someone with the degree they want. Have them ask the company to pay the way through school while they work for them. Many companies pay tuition for their "adult" employees; just reverse it on them. Will they all say yes? Absolutely not; in fact, most will say no, but it only takes one yes, so ask often.

Look into companies that have work-study programs. Many companies offer to pay for school and have struck tuition deals with local colleges to attract a labor force. UPS, for instance, has a program in many cities where you can work

twenty hours per week sorting boxes at night, and they will pay your tuition for school during the day. Plus, they tend to pay you very well for part-time work. That is just one example of many. This type of program is for someone who wants the knowledge, not to go to school just for the "college experience," which translates into: They want to party. If you want to go into debt to teach your kids to drink beer or for them to get a pedigree, you need more than a simple Total Money Makeover.

Look into what the military has to offer. The military isn't for everyone, but a young man who used to work for me got a free college education by serving four years in the army. Honestly, he hated the army, but it was his ticket to school. He grew up in subsidized housing and was told all his life that college was not in his future. He just wouldn't be denied.

My mom was the traditional stay-at-home mom, and my father was a garbage man all his life. Although he never went beyond the eighth grade, and my mom never obtained a higher education, my parents are pretty comfortable right now in

their retirement years. Why? Because they didn't believe in debt, and my father is a major cheapskate and passed that wonderful trait on to me. They also emphasized going to college while I was growing up, and that's what I did.

During that time, I drifted from relationship to relationship, partied, and had a good time (or so I thought). Then I became pregnant, and the father didn't want the "responsibility" of raising a child, so I went at it alone.

That was the lowest point in my life. I never felt more alone or ashamed. After I stopped feeling sorry for myself, I looked at different options and got a burning desire to succeed. Why shouldn't I be successful just because I was a single parent? I refused to go back on welfare and live off the system the rest of my life. I decided to go back to college for my master's degree in community counseling. I didn't have any scholarships or money set aside for college, so I joined the Air Force ROTC program to make it happen.

A few years later, out of the blue, a really special friend wrote to me after not hearing from him in eight years and told me that he'd never forgotten me. Well, the rest is history. Joe and I eventually got married, he became a great father to my older son, and two years ago we had another one. Then we started Dave Ramsey's Total Money Makeover plan. We sat down and completed a budget. Since then, Joe and I have paid off $18,000 of debt in eighteen months. Except for our house, we owe $14,000 more to student loans and expect that to be paid off by next year at the latest. We're determined to be millionaires so we are able to give, give, and give back for what we were given. If you have a dream like going to college, there are ways to make it happen!

> *Kelly Pica-Bosco (age 30)*
> *First Lieutenant Air Force Officer*

If full-time military service isn't for you, check out the National Guard. They will pay you to go to boot camp one summer between high school and college and will then pay for enough tuition and books to get you through the rest of the time. Of course, you will serve your country in the National Guard.

Take a high-rejection, high-paying summer sales job. There are countless stories of young people selling books or participating in similar programs to get through school. Some of these young guerrilla-combat salespeople get more of an education in the summer trenches than they do in marketing class. A friend of mine made $40,000 selling in one summer. Upon returning to class in the fall, his marketing professor gave him a C on a sales presentation he did in front of the class. My friend, being immature, asked the professor what he made a year. After some goading, the professor admitted to an income of $35,000 per year. My friend walked out and, sadly, he quit school. He will be okay though; his income last year was over $1,200,000. I don't tell the story to say it is good to be immature and quit school, because even he would tell you he wishes he had finished. I tell that true story because it illustrates that he learned very valuable lessons about marketing while trying to pay for school. There are benefits beyond just the money awaiting the young person who works to pay for all or part of college.

If you already have the student loans or don't want to get a loan in the first place, look into the "underserved areas" programs. The government will pay for school or pay off your student loans if you will go to work in an underserved area. These areas are typically rural or inner-city areas. Most of these programs are for law and medicine. If you are in nursing,

Dave Rants . . .

If you get a big tax refund, you've just allowed the government to use your money interest free for one year.

work a few years in an inner-city hospital with the less fortunate, and you will get a free education, courtesy of the federal government.

Probably my favorite method of funding school, other than saving for it, is unclaimed scholarships. There is more than $4 billion in unclaimed scholarship money every year. These scholarships are not academic or athletic scholarships either. They are of small- to medium-sized dollar amounts from organizations like community clubs. The Rotary Club, the Lions Club, or the Jaycees many times have $250 or $500 per year they award to some good young citizen. Some of these scholarships are based on race or sex or religion. For instance, they might be designed to help someone with Native American heritage get an education.

The lists of these scholarships can be bought on-line, and there are even a few software programs you can purchase. Denise, a listener to my show, took my advice, bought one of the software programs, and worked the system. That particular software covered more than 300,000 available scholarships. She widened the database search until she had 1,000 scholarships to apply for. She spent the whole summer filling out applications and writing essays. She literally applied for 1,000 scholarships. Denise was turned down by 970, but she got 30, and those 30 scholarships paid her $38,000. She went to school for free while her next-door neighbor sat and whined that no money was available for school and eventually got a student loan.

If you walk your way up these Baby Steps, you can send your kids to school without debt. Even if you start late, perseverance and resourcefulness can get them through school. If you want to go to college badly enough in America today, you can. The good news is that those of you who have a Total Money Makeover will likely not only pay for your child's education, but also—by teaching your children to handle money, and by becoming wealthy—your grandchildren can go to school debt-free.

11

Pay Off the Home Mortgage: Be Ultrafit

I have a good friend who runs marathons. I sit and listen in awe to the stories of the marathons he has run. I sit and listen in awe to the dedication, training, and pain marathoners embrace. To think of running 26.2 miles is hard for a guy who sees 2.6 miles as a real daily accomplishment. Marathoners are some of the fittest people on the planet. As you reach Baby Step Six, you reach marathoner status in the wealth-building world. You have run the good race, but you aren't done.

Bruce, my marathon friend, tells me that at about the eighteen-mile mark (out of 26.2) runners begin to lock up. Some really nasty things start to happen to your muscles and your mind at that point. Almost through the race and nothing wants to finish. The highly trained and conditioned body starts talking to you about stopping. Big black clouds of doubt enter the mentally tough and trained competitive mind. You begin to think things like, *Eighteen miles is pretty good; few others could accomplish that.* If you aren't really careful, "The Good Enough" can become the enemy of "The Best." "Bad" is seldom the enemy of "The Best," but mediocrity with a dose of doubt can keep you from excellence. Finishing well can be more important than starting well.

> If you aren't really careful, "The Good Enough" can become the enemy of "The Best."

183

Reach for the Gold Ring

At this point in your Total Money Makeover, you are debt-free except the house, and you have three to six months of expenses ($10,000+/–) saved for emergencies. At this point in your Total Money Makeover, you are putting 15 percent of your income into retirement savings and you are investing for your kid's college education with firm goals in sight on both. You are now one of the top 5 to 10 percent of Americans because you have some wealth, have a plan, and are under control. At this point in your Total Money Makeover, you are in grave danger! You are in danger of settling for "The Good Enough." You are at the eighteen-mile mark of a marathon, and now that it is time to reach for the really big gold ring, the final two Baby Steps could seem out of your reach. Let me assure you that many have been at this point. Some have stopped and regretted it; others have stayed gazelle-intense long enough to finish the race. The latter have looked and seen just one major hurdle left, after which they can walk with pride among the ultrafit who call themselves financial marathoners. They can count themselves among the elite who have finished The Total Money Makeover.

About three years ago, I spent my lunch hour purchasing a dining room set on my credit card. At this point in my life, I was totally ignorant of the fact that I was purchasing things that I didn't need and couldn't afford. My husband and I paid on two cars, a personal loan, and spent every penny we made each week!

In the same year, I found The Dave Ramsey Show *on the radio. "Are you sick of living like 'normal' people?" Dave asked on the radio. I instantly replied out loud, "Yes, yes, yes!" I begged my husband to attend one of Dave's "Live Events" in our city later that month. What a miracle! By the first break, my husband had emotionally arrived at the same place I was! We sat at this seminar with debt, no savings for college, and very little retirement savings, but we walked out with hope; hope that, together, we could turn around and win at this thing called "finances."*

Well, it's been three years, and we are debt-free, except for the mortgage! It took only fourteen months to pay off $26,000 in debt! We have a fully funded emergency fund, the appropriate level of term life insurance, a refinanced fifteen-year mortgage, and a zero-based budget that includes a large amount for college savings. We save 15 percent for retirement, and the tithes that we have always given now include substantial giving!

Can I put into words the feeling of security I have with no debt and savings to boot? Could I explain to someone how, because our financial situation was secure, money was not an issue when we said "yes" to a sixteen-year-old nephew whose father had become ill and needed a new home to live in? And later when a twelve-year-old child in our church needed a foster home?

So back to the first day I heard The Dave Ramsey Show. *My husband and I had two children, $26,000 in debt, a small amount of Whole Life insurance, a thirty-year mortgage, and no idea where our money was going. Look at us now! We are now a six-member family who, in unison, say, "Thank You, God!" and "Thank you, Total Money Makeover!" Now it's time to pay off the mortgage!*

Sheila Breeden (age 39)
Administrative Assistant

Baby Step Six:
Pay Off Your Home Mortgage

The final hurdle before you turn the corner for the last few miles is to become completely debt-free. No payments. How would it feel to have no payments? I have said it before, and I will repeat myself until you hear me; if you invested what you pay in monthly payments, you'd be a debt-free millionaire before long. Your largest wealth-building tool is your income; you have read that over and over. Now you get to see the possibilities unfold. You have trained, conditioned, and eaten right to run this marathon, so don't quit on the eighteenth mile! Every dollar in your budget that you can find above living, retirement, and college should be used to make extra payments on your home. Attack that home mortgage with gazelle intensity.

> How would it
> feel to have no
> payments?

My family has a fabulous dog, a Chinese pug, a dog like Frank in the *Men in Black* movies. Her name is Heaven, and when we talk to her she cocks her little round head sideways in a questioning look as if we have lost our minds. If you heard the way we talk to the dog, you might think we really had lost our minds. We have all seen the cocked-sideways look coming at us when we have said something weird, something against the culture. When I say, "Pay off the mortgage," some of you look at this book as if I had told you to build wings and fly to the moon.

Anytime I speak about paying off mortgages, people give me that special look. They think I'm crazy for two reasons. One, most people have lost their hope, and they don't really believe there is any chance for them. Two, most people believe all the mortgage myths that have been spread. Yes, we must dispel a few more myths. There are two really big "reasons" that keep seemingly intelligent people (like me for years) from paying off mortgages, so we will start with those.

Remember, Beware of the Myths

Big Reason Number One:

Myth: **It is wise to keep my home mortgage to get the tax deduction.**

Truth: **Tax deductions are no bargain.**

We discussed tax-deduction math when we looked at car fleeces. Let's review. If you have a home with a payment of around $900, and the interest portion is $830 per month, you have paid around $10,000 in interest that year, which creates a tax deduction. If, instead, you have a debt-free home, you would in fact lose the tax deduction, so the myth says keep your home mortgaged because of tax advantages.

This situation is one more opportunity to discover if your CPA can add. If you do not have a $10,000 tax deduction and you are in a 30 percent bracket, you will have to pay $3,000 in taxes on that $10,000. According to the myth, we should send $10,000 in interest to the bank so we don't have to send $3,000 in taxes to the IRS. Personally, I think I will live debt-free and not make a $10,000 trade for $3,000. However, any of you who want $3,000 of your taxes paid, just e-mail me and I will personally pay $3,000 of your taxes as soon as your check for $10,000 clears into my bank account. I can add.

Big Reason Number Two:

Myth: **It is wise to borrow all I can on my home (or continually refinance for cash out) because of the great interest rates; then I can invest the money.**

Truth: **You really don't make anything when the smoke clears.**

This one is a little complicated, but if you follow me, you will have intellectually grasped why so many people have fallen into a financial pit. The myth that I was taught in academia (I am not against higher learning, by the way, as long as we are learning the truth) is to use lower-interest debt to invest in higher-return investments. Sadly, some "Financial Planners" have told Americans to borrow on their homes at around 8 percent to invest in good growth-stock mutual funds averaging 12 percent because you make an easy 4 percent spread.

Mutual funds are awesome investments, and as I have said, I personally have tons of money invested in good growth-stock mutual funds. Also, the stock market has averaged around 12 percent from the beginning. Some years are great and some are lousy, and we have had both in the last ten years, but the long-term average is around 12 percent. So I buy and recommend mutual funds.

The problem with this myth is that the assumptions used to get to that 4 percent spread or profit on investing are wrong. Mythsayers, and I have been one, are very naive in how they approach investing.

Let's look at borrowing $100,000 on your home to invest. If you borrowed at 8 percent, you would pay $8,000 in interest, and if you invested the $100,000 you borrowed on your home and made 12 percent, you would make $12,000 in return, netting you $4,000. Or would you? Where I live, if you make $12,000 on an investment, you will pay taxes. If you are in a

Myths vs. Truth

Myth: By cosigning a loan, I am helping a friend or relative.

Truth: Be ready to repay the loan; the bank wanted a cosigner for a reason.

30 percent bracket, you will pay $3,600 in taxes at ordinary income rates or $2,400 if you invest at capital gains rates. So you will not net $4,000, but instead $400 to $1,600. But we aren't through yet.

If I own the home next to you and have no debt, and you (because of your investment adviser guy) borrowed $100,000 on your home, who has taken more risk? When the economy moves south, when there is war or rumors of war, when you get sick or have a car wreck or are downsized, you will run into major problems with a $100,000 mortgage that I will never have. So debt causes risk to increase.

Since debt causes increased risk, we must mathematically factor in a reduction in return if we are sophisticated investors. If you can make 12 percent on a mutual fund, and I try to get you to invest in a bet on the roulette wheel, which will return you 500 percent, you would automatically say the two don't compare. Why? Risk.

Dave Rants . . .

When your spouse gets the raise you are expecting, don't raise your lifestyle with it. Save more! Invest more!

Common sense tells you not to compare mutual funds and roulette wheel returns without adjusting the returns for risk. Common sense tells you to discount the 500 percent upside of the roulette wheel because of risk. After discounting the roulette wheel for risk, you would rather have the mutual fund. Good choice.

Actually this is done in academia as well. There is a statistical measure of risk called a beta. A big beta means a big risk. Graduate-level financial people are taught mathematical formulas to make risky investments compare apples to apples with safer investments after adjustment for risk. We just never apply that formula to a debt-free home versus a mortgaged and invested home, which is very naive. The technical formula is great for putting you to sleep, but understand that you can't compare risk with no risk unless you make adjustments.

The bottom line is that after adjusting for taxes and risk, you don't make money on our little formula. Throughout a lifetime of investing and mortgaging, the debt-free person will actually come out ahead. Maybe not this year, maybe not next, but on the whole, life will teach you about risk, and the debt-free will like what they learn better than those who try to make this "easy" 4 percent.

When you pay off your home and you have no payments, try something. Sit down on your paid-for back porch and take off your paid-for shoes. Now stand up and walk across your paid-for grass in the backyard. It feels different! Common sense.

Myth: **Take out a thirty-year mortgage and promise yourself to pay it like a fifteen-year, so if something goes wrong you have wiggle room.**

Truth: **Something will go wrong.**

One thing I am sure of in my Total Money Makeover, I had to quit telling myself that I had innate discipline and fabulous natural self-control. That is a lie. I have to put systems and programs in place that make me do smart things. Saying, "Cross my fingers and hope to die I promise, promise, promise I will pay extra on my mortgage because I am the one human on the planet who has that kind of discipline," is kidding yourself. A big part of

> Know where you are weak, and take action to make sure you don't fall prey to the weakness.

being strong financially is that you know where you are weak and take action to make sure you don't fall prey to the weakness. And we ALL are weak.

Sick children, bad transmissions, prom dresses, high heat bills, and dog vaccinations come up, and you won't make the extra payment. Then we extend the lie by saying, "Oh, I will next month." Grow up! The FDIC says that 97.3 percent of people don't systematically pay extra on their mortgage.

Shorter Terms Matter

Purchase Price	$130,000	
Down Payment	<u>$ 20,000</u>	
Mortgage Amount	$110,000	
At **7%** Interest Rate		
30 Years	**$732**	**$263,520**
15 Years	<u>**$988**</u>	<u>**$177,840**</u>
Difference	**$256**	**$ 85,680**

Two hundred fifty dollars more per month, and you will save almost $100,000 and fifteen years of bondage. The really interesting thing I have observed is that fifteen-year mortgages always pay off in fifteen years. Again, part of a Total Money Makeover is putting in place systems that automate smart moves, which is what a fifteen-year mortgage is. Thirty-year mortgages are for people who enjoy slavery so much they want to extend it for fifteen more years and pay thousands of dollars more for the privilege. If you must take out a mortgage, pretend only fifteen-year mortgages exist.

If you have a great interest rate, it is not necessary to refinance to pay a mortgage off in fifteen years or earlier. Simply make payments as if you have a fifteen-year mortgage, and your mortgage will pay off in fifteen years. If you want to pay any mortgage off in twelve years or any number you want, visit my Web site or get a calculator and calculate the proper payment at your interest rate on your balance for a twelve-year mortgage (or the number you want). Once you have that payment amount, add to your monthly mortgage payment the difference between the new principal and interest payment and your current principal and interest payment, and you will pay off your home in twelve years.

The best time to refinance is when you can save on interest. Use the worksheets on the following pages to determine whether you should refinance. When refinancing, paying points or origination fees are not in your best interest. Points or origination fees are prepaid interest. When you pay points you get a lower Annual Percentage Rate (APR) because you have already paid some of the interest up front. The math shows that you don't save enough on interest rates to pay yourself back for the points. When you pay points you are prepaying interest and it takes an average of about 10 years to get your money back. The Mortgage Bankers Association says the average life of a mortgage is only about 5.6 years, so on average you don't save enough to get your money back before you pay the loan off by moving or refinancing. When refinancing, ask for a "par" quote, which means zero points and zero origination fee. The mortgage broker can make a profit by selling the loan; they don't need the origination fee to be profitable.

Myth: **It is wise to use the lower rates offered by an ARM mortgage or balloon mortgage if you know you'll "be moving in a few years anyway."**

Truth: **You will be moving when they foreclose.**

The ARM, Adjustable Rate Mortgage, was invented in the early 1980s. Prior to that, those of us in the real estate business sold fixed-rate 7 or 8 percent mortgages. What happened? I was there in the middle of that disaster of an economy when fixed-rate mortgages went as high as 17 percent and the real estate world froze. Lenders paid out 12 percent on CDs but had money loaned out at 7 percent on hundreds of millions of dollars in mortgages. They were losing money, and lenders don't like to lose money. So the Adjustable Rate Mortgage was

Addendum One

How to Figure Your New Payment
Monthly Payment per $1,000 in Loan Amount

Rate	15-Year	30-Year
4.5%	7.65	5.07
5.0%	7.91	5.37
5.5%	8.17	5.68
6.0%	8.44	6.00
6.5%	8.71	6.32
7.0%	8.99	6.66
7.5%	9.28	7.00
8.0%	9.56	7.34
8.5%	9.85	7.69
9.0%	10.15	8.05
9.5%	10.44	8.41
10.0%	10.75	8.78
10.5%	11.05	9.15
11.0%	11.37	9.52
11.5%	11.68	9.90
12.0%	12.00	10.29

_____ \ 1,000 = _____ X _____ = _____

Sale Price \ 1,000 =   #1000's   X   Factor   = Monthly Pymt

Example: Sale Price - $90,000, 15 years at 8%

$90,000 \1,000 = 90 X 9.56 (look at rate and # of years financed) =

$860.40 Monthly Payment

Addendum Two
Should I Refinance?

Current Principal and Interest Payment   _____
(without taxes & insurance)

New Principal and Interest Payment (minus)   _____

Equals Monthly Savings   _____

_____ / _____ = _____

Total Closing Costs Divided by Savings = Number of Months to Break Even

Example: Refinance on a $90,000 mortgage

$1,100 current payment - $950 new payment = $150 savings
$1,950 closing cost divided by $150 savings = 13 months

Will you stay in your home longer than the number of months to break even? If so, you are a candidate for a refinance.

ESTIMATED CLOSING COSTS TABLE

Loan Amount	Closing Costs	Loan Amount	Closing Costs
30,000	1,500	35,000	1,550
40,000	1,600	45,000	1,650
50,000	1,700	55,000	1,725
60,000	1,775	65,000	1,800
70,000	1,825	75,000	1,850
80,000	1,900	85,000	1,925
90,000	1,950	95,000	1,975
100,000	2,000	150,000	2,300
200,000	2,600	250,000	2,900

Addendum Three

How to Figure the Change in Your ARM

Your Adjustable Rate Mortgage adjusts based on the movement of an index. You can find your index in your original note or mortgage. The most commonly used index is the Treasury Bill. The one-year ARM uses the one-year T-Bill, and the three-year ARM uses the three-year T-Bill, and so on. Other commonly used indexes are the LIBOR and THE 11TH DISTRICT COST OF FUNDS.

First, find out what index you use and when it is adjusted.

Next, find out (also from your paperwork) what "margin" was assigned to your loan (usually 2.59).

Basically your ARM moves as the index moves.

The index is usually published daily in the *Wall Street Journal.*

So if you have a one-year ARM that adjusts with the one-year T-Bill and a margin of 2.59 (which is typical), then at the one-year anniversary of your closing you would look up the one-year T-Bill in the *Wall Street Journal.* Add the T-Bill to your margin, and you have your new rate (if it is not capped).

Example: T-Bill 4.41 plus margin 2.59 = 7% new interest rate.

Warning: Almost all ARMs start below margin the first year, guaranteeing a payment increase at anniversary unless rates DROP.

born, in which your interest rate goes up when the prevailing market interest rates go up. The ARM was born to transfer the risk of higher interest rates to you, the consumer. In the last several years, home mortgage rates have been at a thirty-year low. It is not wise to get something that adjusts when you are at the bottom of rates! The mythsayers always seem to want to add risk to your home, the one place you should want to make sure has stability.

Balloon mortgages are even worse. Balloons pop, and it is always strange to me that the popping sound is so startling. Why don't we expect it? It is in the very nature of balloons to pop. Wise financial people always move away from risk, and the balloon mortgage creates risk nightmares. When your entire mortgage is due in thirty-six or sixty months, you send out engraved invitations for Murphy (Remember him? If it can go wrong, it will) to live in your spare bedroom. I have seen hundreds of clients and callers over the years like Jill.

Jill is the wife of a sophisticated, upwardly mobile corporate guy.

> ### SHOCKING STATS
>
> 80% of Americans believe their standard of living will go up at retirement. Talk about living in a fantasy!

Her husband assured her they would be moving up because his career was on the fast track. So they got the lower interest rate and took a five-year balloon. "We just knew we would move inside five years," she said. Her husband began having headaches in the third year of the mortgage, which, sadly, they discovered were caused by a brain tumor. We met this upwardly mobile corporate executive with limited speech and in a wheelchair, totally and permanently disabled at thirty-eight years of age. His life had been spared, but the surgeries had devastated him. Jill, now a middle-aged mom of two with a disabled husband, didn't have the income to refinance the home when the balloon came due.

The bank wasn't evil; they were just doing their job as they began foreclosure. I wish I could tell you a happy ending, but the truth is, they sold their home at a deep discount to stop the foreclosure and now rent and try to survive. All of this happened because they tried to save a few dollars on the interest rate, "and we knew were going to move." They did.

Myth: **The home equity loan is good to have instead of an emergency fund.**

Truth: **Again, emergencies are precisely when you don't need debt.**

The home equity loan is one of the most aggressively marketed loans today. The average American in debt to his eyeballs has exhausted all means of borrowing except the big second mortgage on his home. This is very sad because we now put our homes at risk to go on vacation, open a business, consolidate debt, or just for an emergency fund. Families come to us in dire straits when the home equity loan is their last bad mistake and the straw that breaks the camel's back.

The banking industry calls these loans HELs for short, and my experience tells me they simply left off an *L*. These loans are very dangerous, and an unbelievable amount of them end in foreclosure.

Even a conservative person who doesn't have credit-card debt and pays cash for vacations can make the mistake of the HEL by setting up a loan or a "line of credit" just for emergencies. That seems reasonable until you have walked through an emergency or two, and you realize very plainly that an emergency is the last time you need to be borrowing money. If you have a car wreck or lose your job and then borrow $30,000 against your home to live on while you make a comeback, you will likely lose your home. Most HELs are renewable annually, meaning they requalify you for the loan once a year.

Ed and Sally didn't realize this. Ed is a very sophisticated financial guy, or so he thought, so he had a HEL for emergencies. Sally had a bad car wreck, and within three months Ed got downsized. They quickly went through the HEL and then got behind in their bills. The annual renewal came up on the HEL, and the bank chose not to renew their loan because of their bad credit, which had been perfect for the previous seventeen years of marriage. The bank called the note. Ed couldn't believe the bank would kick them when they were down. The note being called meant they had to refinance to pay off the bank, but guess what? They couldn't because their credit was bad. The end result was very sad; they sold their home to avoid a foreclosure. Ed was wrong. They should have had an emergency fund instead of a loan.

Myth: You can't pay cash for a home!

Truth: Bet me.

First, let me tell you that mortgage debt is the only kind of debt I don't yell about. I want you to pay off your home as a part of your Total Money Makeover, and, for all the reasons stated in the previous pages, you have to be very careful. When asked about mortgages I tell everyone never to take more than a fifteen-year fixed-rate loan, and never have a payment of over 25 percent of your take-home pay. That is the most you should ever borrow.

I don't borrow money—ever. Luke called me from Cleveland to tell me that some of our listeners and readers are doing what Sharon and I have done, "The 100 Percent Down Plan." Pay cash. Most people don't think that can be done. Luke did it.

Luke made really good money. His income at twenty-three years old was $50,000, and he married a young lady making $30,000. His grandfather had preached to him never to borrow money. So Luke and his new bride lived in a very small apartment over a rich lady's garage. They paid only $250 a month for it. They lived on nothing, did nothing that cost money, and they saved. Man, did they save! Making

$80,000 in the household, they saved $50,000 a year for three years and paid cash for a $150,000 home. They closed on the home on Luke's wife's twenty-sixth birthday. They lived like no one else, and now they are living like no one else. If you make $80,000 per year and don't have any payments, you can become very wealthy very quickly. Keep in mind though, that Luke's friends and relatives thought he should be committed. They made fun of his cars, his lifestyle, and his dream. Only his bride and his grandfather believed in his dream. Who cares what the broke people think?

> Paying cash for a home is possible, very possible.

You may not make $80,000 per year, but you may not need a $150,000 home as your starter either. You may not make $80,000 per year, so your dream might take five years instead of three like Luke's. Ask any eighty-year-old if five years of sacrifice is worth it to change your financial destiny for the rest of your life! Ask any eighty-year-old if five years of sacrifice is worth it to have the satisfaction of knowing you changed your family tree. Paying cash for a home is possible, very possible. What's hard to find is people willing to pay the price in sacrificed lifestyle.

My story begins with the usual sacrifices that most financial accomplishments tend to face. One of the most compelling financial principles that Dave Ramsey exemplifies in his work is that there is a need to set audacious financial goals with the conviction to persevere. By the time I turned twenty-six years old, I had saved enough money to pay cash for a new house.

The true nature of how I handle money was instilled in me at an early age. My parents came from very poor families where they were *not always able to have their basic needs met. They learned to be content with what they had. Unlike the philosophies of today, my sister and I had to learn to be patient. There was never instant gratification; we had to first learn to want what we have and not always to have what we want.*

When I was nineteen, I could have borrowed money and bought a ski boat or a sports car like several of my friends did. However, I chose to save my money in the pursuit of building a house. At the time, my gross income was around $10,000 per year.

I worked thirty to forty hours a week while going to school full-time. It was nothing for me to finish work at 2:00 A.M. and start again at 8:00 A.M. The good that came from my schedule was that I was too busy working to have time to spend money. My personal and business expenditures averaged less than $6,000 a year for over five years.

The hardest part about saving for me was to focus my efforts to save on something that seemed impossible. To combat the problem, I had to come up with a creative plan to keep myself motivated. I copied the floor plan for my house and divided it into squares, with each square representing $1,000 toward the true cost of the house.

By the time I turned twenty-six, with an average income of $44,000, I had saved enough money to pay cash for a house, and the patience had finally paid off. After working and saving money for three years, I built a $135,000 house with cash.

Saving for a house and not having to deal with house payments has allowed my wife and me a tremendous amount of freedom.

John Lambert (age 30)
Residential Real Estate

A Picture of Freedom

Well, there it is, Baby Step Six, debt-free and loving it. Our observation of families who stay gazelle-intense is that they pay off the mortgage about seven years from the date they declared war on the culture, from the date they decided to have a Total Money Makeover. I'm sure by now you are reassured that this is not a get-rich-quick book. What kind of author would tell a microwave culture that it takes an average of seven years to reach the last Baby Step? What kind of author would tell a sound-bite culture that the first two steps take a very tough two or two

and a half years? An author who has seen it done tens of thousands of times by ordinary people with extraordinary desire would do that, the same author who tells you it's not easy, just worth it.

I have used the emotional tag with radio audiences and live audiences that the grass will feel different under your feet when you own it. When you pay off the mortgage, have a barefoot mortgage-burning party and invite all your friends,

> ### Dum Math & Stupid Tax
>
> **Finally, Surfing the Net Pays Off**
> More than $4 billion worth of non-academic or nonathletic scholarships are unclaimed every year (Now that's really dumb!) Putting your college-bound teen to work searching for scholarships could end up paying thousands (or even tens of thousands) of dollars toward college tuition. Isn't that worth giving up TV, chat rooms, or X-box a few hours per week?

relatives, and neighbors. Maybe they will catch the bug and want a Total Money Makeover when they see yours is really working.

Were you to visit my offices, you would find around our meeting room mementos of people having a Total Money Makeover. There are lots of exhibits built of destroyed and maimed credit cards sent in by people who have discovered if they *will* live like no one else, later they *can* live like no one else. One of the more memorable exhibits is a framed letter with a zip-lock bag. This letter and sample of fescue were handed to me in person in a shopping mall in Louisville, Kentucky. I was there doing a radio appearance and book signing when up walked Alicia, or "Al," as she likes to be called.

According to her letter, Al's story was typical but didn't end normally. She and her husband started their Total Money Makeover at age twenty-five. They listened to me on our talk radio show and decided they'd had enough. They started with $20,000 in student loans, $10,000 in car loans, $3,000 in credit-card debt, and an $85,000 mortgage; a grand total of $118,000 in debt. On a $70,000 annual household income, they paid off every red cent in six years. At thirty-one years young, Al stood before me a smiling and free woman. She brought me one of my favorite gifts, too. She brought me the letter and a zip-lock bag. What was in the bag? Fescue from her backyard, "because," she said, "the grass really does feel different under my bare feet in the backyard now that there is no mortgage and we are DEBT-FREE!"

I asked what she was going to do now that she was debt-free. Her response was fun. She said she and her husband were going to dinner to celebrate. At dinner they were going to do two things: first, read the menu from left to right for a change, because money is now no object. Second, at the celebration dinner they fully intended to spend more than a car payment! You see, if you will live like no one else, later you can live like no else.

Next, Al said she and her husband were on a direct course to the last Baby Step and would give more than they had ever imagined they would have. At thirty-one, this couple is destined for extreme levels of wealth. Congratulations, Al. You and your husband are true examples of what a Total Money Makeover looks like.

12

Build Wealth Like Crazy:
Arnold Schwarzedollar, Mr. Universe of Money

You have reached that perfect number, Baby Step Seven. By reaching the last step of your Total Money Makeover, you have entered the top 2 percent of Americans. You are totally debt-free—no house payment, no car payment. You are not Mastered by a Card, you have not Discovered bondage, American Excess has left your life, you have no student loans (your old pet), and you are free. You live on a monthly written plan and agree on it with your spouse, if you're married. You have a retirement destiny that looks considerably better than Alpo and Social Insecurity. If you have children, they will be students without a student loan. You have lived like no one else, so now you will be able to live like no one else. Through sweat and sacrifice, you have reclaimed control of your life and your most powerful wealth-building tool, your income.

Baby Step Seven:
Build Wealth

What was the purpose of your having a Total Money Makeover? Why did you do it? Why all the sacrifice and work? To be in debt and out of control doesn't take nearly as much effort. Why go to all this trouble? Why do you want to have wealth? If you think wealth will answer all

203

life's questions and make you trouble-free, you are delusional. I have had wealth twice in my life, and I don't find it to be trouble-free; as a matter of fact, most of the troubles have zeros on them. Wealth is not

> Wealth is not an escape mechanism. It is instead a tremendous responsibility.

an escape mechanism. It is instead a tremendous responsibility. So what would you do if you had $18 million that it took you forty years to acquire?

After years of studying, teaching, and even preaching on this subject across America, I can find only three good uses for money. Money is good for FUN. Money is good to INVEST. And money is good to GIVE. Most anything else you find to do with it doesn't represent good mental and spiritual health on your part. So if you one day have $18 million, you should do all three of these things. In fact, while you are working the steps to wealth, you should be doing all three of these things. You have lost weight, you have built up your cardiovascular system, and now you have added muscle because you have lost the debt, saved for emergencies, and invested long-term for retirement and college planning. At this stage in The Total Money Makeover, you are Arnold Schwarzedollar, Mr. Universe of Money, with serious abs, pecs, and quads. You have all this financial muscle, so now you should do something intentional with it. It is not just to look at. We built this financial superbody for a reason. To have *FUN, INVEST,* and *GIVE.*

Yes, We Get to Have Fun

The kid in us likes the FUN part of this equation, and since we have made this kid behave for a long time with promises of ice cream if he does so, he should get some ice cream. Should anyone wear a $30,000 watch? Should anyone drive a brand-new $50,000 car? Should anyone live in a $700,000 home? Absolutely; they should. The problem with people is, they buy those things when they can't afford them.

In Chapter 3 on Debt Myths, we talked about new cars and what a bad investment they are. They go down in value very rapidly. Because the new car is the largest thing we buy that goes down in value, the car payment is usually our largest payment, except for the home mortgage. Roughly 70 percent of the people I assist in a Total Money Makeover have to make the difficult decision to sell their car so they can be free of the big payment. If they don't free themselves from this very large debt and very large payment, they find it very hard to climb the Baby Steps. So some days my talk radio show becomes the "sell the car" show. Some days it seems my answer to every question is, "Sell the car." "Don't buy that new car," is advice you will hear from me so often you'll be saying it in your sleep.

Sometimes a caller will ask if he can afford a purchase while on his Total Money Makeover. Sometimes a new listener wanders into the snare of asking about buying something totally ridiculous. I'm nice, at first, to explain that she can't do that now. I'll say something like, "The emergency fund is more important than a leather couch." I have a computer in front of me while I'm on the air, which the phone screener uses to tell me who is on hold and what they are calling about. Not long ago I looked down at the screen and saw that Michael was waiting to talk with me. The note said he wanted to buy a Harley-Davidson motorcycle. Harleys are fabulous bikes, but they are not for broke people, because a nice one will cost over $20,000. I prejudged Michael to be twenty-eight years old, with two car payments, two kids, one wife, and no money. I figured Michael was one of those guys who puts his little-boy fantasies before the good of his family. I loaded

> Dum Math & Stupid Tax
>
> **Home Sweet Loan**
>
> Wish to borrow $100,000 to invest? At 8%, you would pay $8,000 in interest, but if you borrowed $100,000 on your home, you might earn 12% on your investment, netting you $4,000. Or would you? After taxes you may only net $400 to $1,600 while putting your home in great financial risk.

my gun to respond to his question. I was prepared not only to tell him not to buy a Harley, but also to straighten out his whole way of looking at financial matters.

I figured Michael was probably making $48,000 per year and broke, so obviously he had no business buying a $20,000 toy. "Dave, I've always dreamed of owning a Harley," Michael started. "I just called to see if you thought I should buy one, and if I can afford it." For a few minutes I went on about how great Harleys are and how a lot of guys would love to have one. I usually ask a little about the caller's financial situation in order to make a quasi-reasonable judgment, so I asked Michael what he made last year. His response was, "$650,000." "Yeah, but what have you averaged over the last five years?" I asked, thinking he maybe hit the Lotto. "About $550,000 per year," was his answer. Now he had me on the ropes. "So how much do you have in investments?" I queried further. "About $20 million," came his final blow. "Buy the Harley, dude!" was my advice. Can Michael afford a $20,000 toy? Absolutely. Is it morally wrong for him to enjoy a fun item he wants when for him to purchase it as a percentage of his wealth is equal to most people buying a Happy Meal? No, there is absolutely nothing financially or morally wrong with that purchase. The man has earned his Harley and then some.

> ## Myths vs. Truth
>
> **Myth:** I can't use cash because it is dangerous; I might get robbed.
>
> **Truth:** You are being robbed every day by not using the power of cash.

Have some fun!

I told you Michael's story to make sure you understand that one reason to have a Total Money Makeover is to build wealth that allows you to have fun. So have some fun! Taking your family, even the extended ones, on a seven-day cruise, buying large diamonds, or even buying a new car are things you can afford to do when you have millions of dollars. You can afford to do these things because when you do them your money position is hardly even affected. If you like travel, travel. If you like clothes, buy some. I am releasing you to have some fun with your money, because money is to be enjoyed. That guilt-free enjoyment is one of the three reasons to have a Total Money Makeover.

Investing Is How We Keep on Winning

The grown-up inside us likes the INVESTING of money because that is part of what makes you wealthy. Also, the growing dollars are a way of keeping score in our Total Money Makeover game. Are we winning? It truly becomes a game. In the movie *Two Weeks' Notice*, Hugh Grant plays George Ward. The character of George is a very wealthy and spoiled corporate figurehead. His character isn't one we want to imitate, but he has a great line in the movie about his wealth. He is telling Sandra Bullock's character that he lives in this luxury hotel, and he says nonchalantly, "Actually, I own the hotel; my life is a little bit like Monopoly."

Investing can feel like that after a while—"a little bit like Monopoly." When you are playing Monopoly, you can be up, or you can get behind. Sometimes the market fluctuates, but as mature investors we ride out the waves, stay in for the long term. Sometimes I meet people who arrive at this step and are scared because just as they reach retirement age, their investments

> **SHOCKING STATS**
>
> 19% of the people who filed for bankruptcy in 2002 were college students.

are heading down. Never fear; if you have quality investments with long-term track records, they will come back. Besides, you don't need all the nest egg at once to retire on; you just need some of the income from it. So since you don't need it all right then, it would be silly to cash everything out while the market is at the bottom. "Buy high; sell low" is not the formula to wealth. Be patient with the market while living off the income the nest egg produces.

You can choose to be a little more sophisticated, but until you have over $10 million, I would keep your investing very simple. You can clutter your life with a bunch of unnecessary stress by getting into extremely complex investments. I use simple mutual funds and debt-free real estate as my investment mix—very clean, simple, investments with some basic tax advantages. As you arrive at this Baby Step, if you want to own some paid-for real estate, it can be fun.

Always manage your own money.	

Always manage your own money. You should surround yourself with a team of people smarter than you, but you make the decisions. You can tell if they are smarter than you if they can explain complex issues in ways you can understand. If a member of your team wants you to do something "because I say so," get a new team member. You are not hiring a daddy; you are gathering counsel. God did not give them the responsibility over this money. He gave that to you. Celebrities and pro athletes often lose their entire fortunes because they give up the responsibility of managing their own money. The money manager who loses your hard-earned investments won't live with the regret and pain that you will. The Bible states, "In the multitude of counselors there is safety" (Prov. 11:14 NKJV). A good estate-planning attorney, a CPA or tax expert, an insurance pro, an investment pro, and a good realtor are a few of the essential team members you should gather around you. I endorse the use of financial planners if they are team members and not the sole captains of their teams.

When selecting and working with your wealth team, it is vital to bring on only members who have the heart of a teacher, not the heart of a salesman or the heart of an "expert." The salesman is always chasing a commission and thinking short-term, and the "expert" can't help being condescending, which is humorous because they likely have less money than you. Also, when taking advice, evaluate if the person giving the advice will profit from the advice. If your insurance pro is coming up with more great insurance ideas every week, you may have a problem. That is not to say everyone who makes a commission off you is out to get you. There are plenty of commission-only financial people who have extreme levels of integrity. Just be aware of possible conflicts of interest.

My wife and I got married nine years ago and immediately took the advice of some friends to go to a name-brand "Financial Planner." They developed a plan for our goals. The plan included keeping Sharon's two existing mutual funds and her cash reserve, Comprehensive Life insurance, and tax-deferred investing . . . so far, so good. The plan also included some of the "Financial Planner's" own brand-name mutual funds, an annuity, some stock certificates, a Real Estate Investment Trust (REIT), and, you guessed it, Whole Life insurance. Not so good! I looked in my arsenal for weapons to evaluate this plan and found none. Off we go, saving 50 percent of my income toward these "opportunity investments."

Then I stumbled onto Dave Ramsey's radio show and started listening. I immediately realized that Dave is one of the thousands of people who are smarter than I am. My wife gets annoyed with me, as she's been trying to get me to understand these principles all along!

I first realized making Sharon do all the financial decision making and budgeting for the last seven years was irresponsible and wrong. Then I realized that I'd been investing in a bunch of stuff I didn't understand. I began to research mutual funds on the Internet. I told my financial guy I didn't think Whole Life was a good product to own. Then he tried to sell me more! I told him that I didn't understand the REIT and how it worked. Guess what? He really couldn't explain why I owned it or how it worked either. I told him that I wanted out of it, and he didn't even know how to get me out of it! Dave Ramsey's comments on knowing what you're investing in are so true! Investing with someone with "the heart of a teacher" started to sound attractive.

Bam! All of a sudden the whole thing became obvious, so I immediately dumped my "financial adviser" and decided to teach my kids The Total Money Makeover plan early in life!

Bill (age 39)
and Sharon (age 39) Been
Airline Pilot; Stay-at-Home Mom

Within Baby Step Seven: Build Wealth, there is a subsection b, another milestone. The second milestone within becoming wealthy is the "Pinnacle Point."

Growing up in the suburbs in Tennessee, I grew accustomed to riding a bike and facing hills. To a seven-year-old with one gear, a huge hill looked like Mount Everest. I don't know which kid in history did it first, but the technique for small-guy bike hill climbing has been passed down for generations—the switchback. Instead of pedaling straight up, we would painfully go side to side, taking a small bite at a time of our Tennessee mountain. The unpopular players' baseball cards made a slow *click, click, click* through the spokes as we made our ascent. The heat seemed ovenlike, and the beads of sweat turned to rivers. This is the time a seven-year-old pushes with every muscle in his being. The strain and determination show on your face like last year's Halloween mask. You pull on the handlebars with all the power your arm muscles will produce to push your legs down on the pedals one more time. Push, push, breathe, breathe until you finally reach the top.

What do you find at the top? The cynical among us just said, "Another hill to climb." Those of us with a kid still alive inside know what was at the top. Those of us who still have a kid inside who can dream, who can

Dave Rants . . .

Separate checking accounts mean one of two things, either ignorance or problems.

believe, and who can hope know what we found at the top. Those of us that have pushed up some unbelievable hills know what I found that Tennessee summer day at the top of the hill. I found that perfect moment. The perfect moment when you push the pedal the last time before going down a huge hill on the other side. The perfect moment when you hang in the balance, after all the sweat, the work, and the agony, and a smile breaks across your face. That moment just before we take the glorious ride down is the "Pinnacle Point."

And the ride down *is* glorious. The wind blows through your hair, and your feet are not on the pedals anymore but on the handlebars. The *click, click, click* of the baseball cards becomes a chattering with a sound like thousands of crickets. You are now enjoying the ride; the coasting is the fruit of your labors. Memories of strain, sweat, and repeated near failure fade as the sun shines and the wind tickles

The ride down is glorious.

your ears, whispering, "You are the king! You did it! You climbed the hill! You didn't quit! You paid the price to win!" The smile in your soul says, "*Accomplishment.*"

If you are beginning to think I'm being a little overdramatic, so be it. It is hard to describe reaching the "Pinnacle Point" without some emotion. This Baby Step takes us to the point at which your money works harder than you do, the "Pinnacle Point." It is the instant in time where focused gazelle intensity has reached critical mass, and your money takes on a life of its own.

This point is not that you are going to quit life when you get there; you will still manage and direct, but the money thing will have its feet up, and you will be coasting downhill. Wealth will find its way to you. Mistakes on your tax return will be in your favor; the IRS will discover them and send you the money back with interest. Well, that's probably an impossible dream, but you get the idea.

When your money makes more than you do, you are officially wealthy. When you can comfortably live on your investment income, you are financially secure. Money is a hard worker, harder than you. Money never gets sick, never gets pregnant, and is never disabled. Money works twenty-four hours a day, seven days a week. Money gets its job done, and it asks for only directions and a firm master.

> When your money makes more than you do, you are officially wealthy.

You have reached the Pinnacle Point when you can live off 8 percent of your nest egg. Go ahead, multiply your nest egg by .08, and if you can live on that number or that number is more than you make, you are coasting downhill. Congratulations! Your money makes more than you do! If you want to do some calculations on hitting this financial security milestone, you can use the forms on the next few pages. You will be able to calculate what your Pinnacle-Point nest egg is, and then, using all your available income, see how many years it will take you to climb that hill. Believe me, everything is downhill after that. Enjoy the ride.

Giving Is the Biggest Reward of the Entire Workout

The most mature part of who you are will meet the kid inside as you learn to involve yourself in the last use of money, which is to GIVE it away. Giving is possibly the most fun you will ever have with money.

FUN is good, but you will tire of golf and travel, and if you eat enough, lobster starts tasting like soap. INVESTING is good, but going around and around that Monopoly board eventually loses its appeal—especially after you reach the Pinnacle Point. Every mentally and spiritually healthy person I've met has been turned on by giving as long as it didn't mean his own lights got cut off. I can promise you from meeting with literally thousands of millionaires that the thing the healthy ones share in common is a love of GIVING.

Only the strong can help the weak, and that is true of money, too. A toddler is not allowed to carry a newborn; only adults who have the muscular strength to ensure safety should carry babies. If you want to help someone, many times you can't do so without money. The Bible states that pure religion is actually helping the poor, not theorizing over why they are poor (see James 1:27). Margaret Thatcher said, "No one would have remembered the good Samaritan if he hadn't had money." The good Samaritan had a good heart and a heavy enough purse to pay an innkeeper to help take care of the injured man. Money was involved. Money was at its best that day. Money gives power to good intentions. That's why I'm unashamedly in favor of building wealth.

My wife and I listen to Dave Ramsey on the radio as often as possible. When I had just a little more than nineteen years in the army, my wife and I decided that we had to start budgeting. We decided that any additional money would be saved, and nothing would be bought until we had the money to pay for it. Since that time, we have not had an account that was over thirty days old.

When I retired, I was an E9 (Command Sergeant Major), and we decided to continue to live on my old E7 (Master Sergeant) pay. The difference and all my raises went straight to the bank for savings. We never had to make a payment on a house, car, or any piece of furniture. I retired thirty years ago, and we have maintained our budget and debt freedom. We do not owe one penny to anyone. In fact, we owned a house and were able to give it as a gift to our daughter and son-in-law, and they have lived by the same principles ever since. The plan literally put us in a position to give the house to them!

Les Powers (age 79)
Retired Army

Let Go

Sadly, I meet people who try to avoid this third use of money, mistakenly thinking they will end up with more. Eric Butterworth tells of an interesting system used to capture monkeys in the jungle. The captors use heavy glass bottles with long necks. Into each bottle they deposit some sweet-smelling nuts. The aroma of the nuts attracts a monkey to the bottle. When the monkey puts its hand into the bottle to get the nuts, the neck of the bottle is too small for its fist to come back out. The monkey can't take his hand out of the bottle without dropping the nuts, which he is unwilling to do. The bottles are too heavy to carry away, so the monkey becomes trapped by nothing more than greed. We may smile at these foolish monkeys, but how many times has our freedom been taken away by nothing more than our greed.

Most of us have given something at some time or another, but I have seen some really fun things happen when good people become wealthy. When you have your Total Money Makeover, you can do some things with scale. I have one friend who buys seventy-five brand-new bikes for an inner-city ministry every year. He gets these bikes at Christmas, and, in conjunction with a missionary group that knows the families in the area, gives them out one at a time to kids in a subsidized housing project. The project is drug-infested and crime riddled, but for one day a year, those young people see someone who wants nothing in return.

Another pastor friend of mine is involved in a project called Seeds of Kindness. An anonymous member of his congregation gave $50,000 to the congregation members to give away, one $100 bill at a time. The member must not use the gift, the member must receive nothing in return, and it should be given as personally as possible. These $100 bills are given human to human across the city with fabulous results. People who had completely lost faith in God and in the human race are shaken to the core by a simple $100 gift. The givers often report having more fun than the receivers.

Secret Santa

We all have seen these powerful examples of giving. *USA Today* has followed a guy who calls himself Secret Santa at Christmas for several years. Secret Santa walks the streets around Christmastime and gives away $100 bills. Nothing required, nothing expected, and he remains anonymous. Sometimes he gives to people in need, and other times he just gives. Every year he gives away around $25,000 in $100 bills. He started this tradition years ago in his hometown of Kansas City and has moved out across America. He gave in New York after 9/11 and in the Virginia/Washington, D.C., area after the sniper attacks. He just walks around and hands people $100 bills. He gets some fabulous reactions and hears some wonderful stories.

In late winter of 1971, he worked as a salesman, and when his company went broke, Santa found himself broke, too. He slept in his car for eight days and hadn't eaten for two days when he went to the Dixie Diner. He ordered and ate a big breakfast. He waited for the crowd to clear, then acted as if he had lost his wallet. The diner's owner, Tom Horn, who was also the cook, came over near the stool where Santa had been sitting and picked up a $20 bill and said, "Son, you must have dropped this." Santa realized later that Tom had planted that twenty to let him out of a sticky situation with his dignity intact. As he drove away, Santa said, "Thank You, Lord, for that man, and I promise if I ever have money, I will do the same."

In 1999 Santa, now a very successful businessman, looked up Tom Horn, now eighty-five years old, in his home of Tupelo, Mississippi. Santa recounted the story of the hungry young man of 1971 while standing on Tom's porch in a Santa hat. He asked Tom what he thought that $20 would be worth by that time and Tom laughingly said, "Probably $10,000." Santa then handed Tom $10,000 cash in an envelope. Of course, Tom tried to hand it back, but finally Santa won out, so Tom deposited the money in the bank. He said he might need it to take care of his wife, who has Alzheimer's.

Horn says of Secret Santa, "He doesn't want any thanks or praise for what he does. He does it out of the goodness of his heart." After giving to dozens of people this last Christmas, Santa said, "Isn't it fun to lift people up and see the smiles on their faces?" I think I know why this Santa gives. He gives because it is the most fun he can possibly have with money, and you will never know until you try.

Do All Three

There are only three uses for money: FUN, INVESTING, and GIVING. You cannot claim Total Money Makeover status until you do all three. You don't have to buy a Harley, invest millions, or give away $25,000 cash, but you do have to do some of each. And as I said earlier, you should begin doing some of each as you go through the steps. Giving something, even if it is just giving your time by serving soup to the homeless, should start from Baby Step One. Fun also begins there, although it has to be inexpensive fun in the beginning; the fun gets bigger and better as we get higher in the steps. Investing, of course, begins at Baby Step Four (Invest 15 Percent of Your Income in Retirement). You are not getting the full use of and enjoyment of your money unless you do all three.

Someone who never has fun with money misses the point. Someone who never invests money will never have any. Someone who never gives is a monkey with his hand in a bottle. Do some of each, and if you are married, let your spouse have some slack as soon as there is some. After you get past the emergency-fund step, let each other function in the areas you like best. My wife, Sharon, is a natural saver, so she always cheats toward investing. I am a natural spender, so I make sure she has fun. We both enjoy giving.

Please push that pedal one more time. Switchback if you have to; failure is not an option. Push, push! I promise, and the tens of thousands who have reached their Pinnacle Point in their Total Money Makeover promise, at the top of the hill is a glorious ride down. Take that ride with us!

I am a thrill-seeker.

I don't skydive, bungee jump, or swim with sharks. The thrills I seek as a pastor are slightly different.

I seek thrills like going on what I call "search and bless" missions.

From time to time, I stumble across a single mom with three kids and a car with threadbare tires. The thrill I seek is to be able to borrow her car to run an errand. The errand is to drive down to the local tire and lube express and have the oil changed and new tires put on. On the way back, I fill it up with gas and run it through the car wash. Then I hand her the keys and don't say a thing about it.

I seek thrills like being in a restaurant with my ten-year-old daughter and seeing a couple of police officers eating and having extra cash in my pocket to walk over to their table and offer to pay for their meal just to say thanks for all they do in our community. (Can you say "teachable moment" in the life of your child?)

I seek thrills like being able to leave a really good tip at the restaurant Sunday after church instead of being lumped into the category of cheapskate churchgoers that are lousy tippers.

I seek thrills like being able to have financial peace in having my bills paid, my emergency fund in place, my used cars paid for, making monthly deposits into my Roth IRA and my child's education fund, and having enough left over from each paycheck to carry $75 to $100 in cash with me, ready, willing, and able to respond to the needs of people who need a hand up, not a handout.

I am becoming a living sermon illustration that it is more blessed to give than to receive. All these thrills are contingent on my living in a place of financial peace, leaving behind slavery to debt, successfully navigating through the wilderness of cash-flow planning and wise investment, both in the kingdom of God and in my own financial future.

As a pastor, I am concerned that I would be guilty of "spiritual malpractice" if I did not speak into the lives of those whom I shepherd in the area of financial stewardship. The truth shall truly set you free!

David Robertson (age 42)
Pastor

13

Live Like
No One Else

You started this book financially flabby, overweight with debt, out of shape in savings, and in desperate need of a personal trainer. In these pages, you have reviewed how tens of thousands of ordinary people have gotten into great financial shape. This is a book about getting out of debt and into wealth. However, there is a problem with following The Total Money Makeover plan. The problem is simply that it's a "proven plan" because it works. If you follow this system, it *will* work. It will work so well that you are going to become wealthy over the next twenty to forty years. The problem with becoming wealthy is that you stand a chance of becoming enamored with wealth. We can easily start to worship money, especially after we have some.

False Cents of Security

According to Proverbs 10:15, a rich man's wealth can become his walled city. In Bible times the wall around the city was the city's protection from the enemy. If all you get from your wealth is the wrong view of it, wealth will destroy your peace. If you get from your wealth the idea that you are some big deal because you gathered some money, you missed the essence of a Total Money Makeover. The wealthy person who is ruled by his stuff is no more free than the debt-ridden consumer we have picked on throughout the book. Antoine Rivaroli said, "There are men who gain from their wealth only the fear of losing it."

Since you have read many pages learning a wealth-building system from me, you might think that I believe stuff is the answer to happiness, emotional well-being, and spiritual maturity. You would be wrong because I know that is not the case. On the contrary, I see a real spiritual danger to having great wealth. The danger is old-fashioned materialism. In his great book *Money, Possessions, and Eternity,* author Randy Alcorn takes a probing look at materialism. Randy discusses a disease running amuck in America: "Affluenza." Affluenza is a malady that affects some of the affluent and their children. Because some of the affluent and their children seek happiness, solace, and fulfillment in the consuming of stuff, they face a problem. By trying to get stuff to do something it wasn't designed to do, they come up empty and end up depressed and even suicidal. They discover bumper-sticker wisdom: "He who dies with the most toys is still dead." Stuff is wonderful; get some stuff, but don't let the pursuit of wealth become your god.

My wife and I are concerned that our wealth be a blessing and not a curse to our children. So we are tough on our kids regarding work, saving, giving, and spending issues. We expect a lot from them and have since they were small. I am very proud of the character of our children. They, like their parents, aren't perfect, but they are doing well. When one of my kids was a teenager, she complained to me, "Do you know how tough it is being Dave Ramsey's kid? Dad, you are so hard on us, making us buy our own cars, manage our own checkbooks. You cut us no slack." I replied that we are tough on them because one day they will inherit our wealth, and that wealth will either ruin their lives or become a tool for great good.

My kids, you, and I can have good things happen as a result of our Total Money Makeover only *if* we have the spiritual character to recognize that wealth is not the answer to life's questions. We further must recognize that while wealth is very fun, it comes with great responsibility.

> **Wealth is not the answer to life's questions.**

Another paradox is that wealth will make you more of what you are. Let that one soak in for a minute. If you are a jerk and you become wealthy, you will be king of the jerks. If you are generous and you become wealthy, you will be most generous. If you are kind, wealth will allow you to show kindness in immeasurable ways. If you feel guilty, wealth will ensure that you feel guilty for the rest of your life.

The LOVE of Money, Not Money, Is the Root of All Evil

As a Christian, I am amazed how certain political and religious groups have decided that wealth is evil. Many of the heroes of biblical faith, of world history, and of our nation were very wealthy, including King David, Solomon, Job, and most of our Founding Fathers. There is a negative mind-set justifing money mediocrity that is maddening. Wealth is not evil, and people who possess it aren't evil by virtue of the wealth. There are rich jerks and poor jerks. Dallas Willard, in his book *Spirit of the Disciplines,* says to *use* riches is to cause them to be consumed, to *trust* in riches is to count upon them for things they cannot provide, but to *possess* riches is to have the right to say how they will or will not be used.

> **To *possess* riches is to have the right to say how they will or will not be used.**

If you are a good person, it is your spiritual duty to possess riches for the good of mankind. If you are a Christian like me, it is your spiritual duty to possess riches so that you can do with them things that bring glory to God. The bottom line is, if you take the stand that managing wealth is evil or carnal, then by default you leave all the wealth to the evil, carnal people. If wealth is spiritually bad, then good people can't have it, so all the bad people get it. It is the duty of the good people to get wealth to keep it from the bad people, because the good people will do good with it. If we all abandon money because some misguided souls view it as evil, then the only ones with money will be the pornographer, the drug dealer, or the pimp. Simple enough?

To Give You Hope

I think you can tell by now that The Total Money Makeover is more than just a discussion on money issues. The Total Money Makeover makes you face the man or woman in the mirror. Facing that man or woman makes us face emotional, relational, physical, and even spiritual aspects of our lives. The wealthy people that I know who are fulfilled didn't just have a Total *MONEY* Makeover. They had a life makeover. Because personal finance is 80 percent behavior and 20 percent knowledge, you will either make your life over in this process, or you will end up miserable. I'm being very spiritual here at the end, but the spiritual is a legitimate aspect of behavior. I see well-rounded, mature people who become all God designed them to be when they get their money closets cleaned out. God has a plan for your life, and that plan isn't to harm you; it is a plan for your future to give you hope (see Jer. 29:11).

> It is time for you to become a gazelle.

Hope is what I want you to walk away with from this book. Hope that you can be like the people whose stories I told in this book. Hope that you can turn your money troubles into money triumphs. Hope that you can retire with dignity. Hope that you can change your family tree, because by building wealth you leave an inheritance. Hope that you can give money in a way you have never given before. It is time for you to become a gazelle. It is time for you to leave the reading and the classroom behind and apply these principles. They are age-old principles, and they work. Tens of thousands of ordinary people just like you and me have become debt-free and even wealthy using this plan. It isn't magic; it is common sense. The exciting thing is, anyone can do this—*anyone*. Are you next? I hope so.

More Total Money Makeover Stories

My husband was nine months away from navy retirement, and we realized that we needed help in order to be ready financially. We had $20,000 in consumer debt and no prospect of a job outside the navy. We both knew it wouldn't take much to make our finances go downhill quickly. We were overwhelmed. Then we heard about Financial Peace University. We had tried several other classes on finance with little results, so it took several months to convince me to try this plan.

By the time we finished learning the plan, we had Baby Step One done ($1,000 in the bank). We had also paid off two loans, and the Debt Snowball was rolling! The Total Money Makeover has changed the future of our family's finances. I have since made sure all my family has The Total Money Makeover resources. It is changing their lives too. Everyone who knows me can tell you about our life-changing experience. I have taught the course and tell everyone I know about it. Our eighteen-year-old has her emergency fund in place, has $1,000 in a Roth IRA, prepays her auto insurance six months in advance, and tithes faithfully. She's done all of this from a part-time job working for a fast-food chain! If you are even thinking about starting The Total Money Makeover plan, DO IT NOW! As Dave Ramsey says, "It's time to change your family tree."

> *Marie (age 40)*
> *and Vincent (age 40)*
> *Guilliams*
> *Self-Employed;*
> *Retired Navy*

Eighteen months ago, my wife and I were newlyweds with $37,000 in debt! We owed about $8,000 on credit cards and the rest on brand-new cars. We thought we were "SUCCESSFUL"!

We were making about $52,000 a year and had just purchased our first home when we discovered Dave Ramsey's Total Money Makeover *plan. We had been a bit uncomfortable with the new home costs and how much of our money was going out versus how much was coming in. But it was the American way . . . "Everybody has a house payment."*

The Total Money Makeover plan started to make sense. We started on the Baby Steps. I sold my new pickup, plus my hot rod I'd been working on, and bought a $1,500 car. My wife picked up some hours at her second job, and I changed jobs completely to raise my income.

We no longer use credit cards, and we don't buy or do anything unless we can pay cash for it.

Even though we raised our income, we have kept the less expensive of the two new cars. I don't miss the hot rod (well, not that much), and my $1,500 car is as reliable as the new one my wife drives!

In four months, we will be completely debt-free, except for the house!

> *Geoff (age 28)*
> *and Tara (age 29) Evans*
> *Sales Representative;*
> *Claims Adjuster*

Four years ago, I had never heard of Dave Ramsey. My husband and I own a small machine shop, and we both work in it. We usually have a slowdown in revenues at the end of the year every year, but that year it didn't pick up again soon after. As a result, we fell further and further behind in everything. In fact, we were four months behind on my van payment, two months behind on my house payment/utilities, and two to four months behind on our other debts! Collectors called constantly. I never answered the phone. I was so worried and upset I didn't know what to do. I truly thought we were going to have to file bankruptcy.

I thought I was going to have a nervous breakdown over our debt and not being able to pay our bills. I was scared!

My youngest daughter was working on a program called The Total Money Makeover taught by a guy named Dave Ramsey. She just thought it was so awesome and kept telling me about it. One day she played a tape of Dave Ramsey for me. I laughed so hard, and then I cried. I thought, Man, this guy knows what I'm going through. *Then I called Dave's office, not sure whether this was a scam or not, and got information about starting the plan.*

I made up my mind that I was going to follow The Total Money Makeover program to the letter. If Dave said do it, I did it. If Dave said, "Don't do it," I didn't do it.

As a result of this plan, we got current. I came to realize that I had to pay my living expenses first, and then I took care of the creditors second. I had to work with them in different ways, and it didn't happen overnight. But now my property taxes are paid ahead of time instead of after I see my name in the delinquent tax column of the newspaper!

It has taken us four years, but we have paid off $125,000 in debt! Except for our house, we are DEBT-FREE!

Jim (age 58)
and Marquita (age 53) Ector
Machinist; Office Manager

A*bout a year and a half ago, I heard* The Dave Ramsey Show *on the radio. Before hearing it, I thought I was good with money management. Needless to say, Dave's suggestions taught me to "fine-tune" my spending habits. I sold a piece of property and stayed totally focused on my financial goals. As a result, I paid off $50,000 of debt in eighteen months!*

Yes, my family thought I had lost my mind or joined a cult!

After becoming debt-free, I saved all the money I was using to pay off debt. Thank heavens I did, because I found out last week that I owe the IRS as a result of selling the property. But I did not even have to worry about where I was going to get the money. I had the money saved and was able to pay the debt I owed.

Dave Ramsey always points out the fact that the borrower is a servant to the lender. The borrower is also servant to the employer. I was afraid to leave my undesirable employment when I had monthly payments. Now that I am debt-free, I have the opportunity to change my career and share my experience with others. Being debt-free has given me a much-desired feeling of peace.

Deanna Coley (age 44)
Financial Counselor

It was thirteen months ago that my wife and I decided we needed to make a plan to pay off the debt that I had brought into our marriage—a little over $42,000. I had credit cards, a high-interest car payment, five different college loans, and medical bills. Since I am a mortgage broker and have the opportunity to see many people's finances, I knew that my situation was pretty typical. Although I had instructed my customers to do "this" or "that" to restructure their debt and work toward a life of financial freedom, I hadn't done if myself, but getting married showed me that now was certainly the time to get serious about it.

We quickly plunged into The Total Money Makeover plan, learning everything from creating an emergency fund, saving, cash-flow planning, relating with money, dumping debt, and understanding investments. The plan broke it all down.

The thing that got me most excited was changing our family's cash-flow position. Over the next thirteen months, Sarah and I lived by a budget. It gave us peace to know where every dollar was going. The first few months were tough, but then it started to happen. With each debt that was paid off, we became more and more excited. We actually looked forward to paying our bills each month! As we sent off checks to our creditors, we felt a sense of joy and relief. We started to feel the excitement of getting rid of some of those heavy weights around our neck; the debt that was trying to kill us was losing its power.

A huge part of our success is directly related to the fact that we did The Total Money Makeover plan together.

We have learned several things these last thirteen months. First, more money doesn't necessarily solve the problem; money management is the key. Second, women look at money very differently from men. Third, having an accountability partner helps. Sarah and I have kept each other accountable when we have needed to be strong for each other. We had urges to buy things for our house, invest in crazy stocks, buy clothes, take trips. It's just that now we know how to afford them, except for the crazy stocks!

Damian (age 26)
and Sarah (age 27) Mingle
Home Loan Specialist;
Personal Assistant

IF YOU WILL LIVE LIKE NO ONE ELSE, LATER YOU CAN LIVE LIKE NO ONE ELSE IF YOU WILL LIVE LIKE NO O

M y husband and I were never any good at managing money. We married eleven years ago, and we have struggled ever since, living paycheck to paycheck, blaming circumstance and everyone but ourselves for our misfortune!

We were desperate! All our bills were past due. We had borrowed from my parents to the tune of $1,400. We had no idea how we were going to repay this loan or how we could bring our bills current.

Then we started The Total Money Makeover plan.

We immediately began to have garage sales to obtain our $1,000 emergency fund. Now, I have to interject: My husband and I could never agree on financial matters. I could never get him involved with our money situation, so I did not expect him to help us dig our way out of the mess. But he was the one who nearly single-handedly raised our $1,000. Then our truck was repo'ed, but we had our emergency fund in place to retrieve it. We ended up with $2,000 saved by the end of the thirteen weeks.

We tried other financial plans; you name them, and we tried them. The Total Money Makeover has been the only plan able to reach people like us, who were admittedly money stupid! We do not make huge amounts of money, and we have expenses just like everybody, but it took the investment of following the plan, reinforcement of each other, and Dave Ramsey's enthusiasm to teach us how to save and not spend away our income. One of the best parts is that we have not felt deprived, and God has blessed our efforts!

We refinanced our home (which was mortgaged for thirty years) for fifteen years and got out from under all our debt except our mortgage. We now have just over $7,000 in our emergency fund and only have around $13,000 to go to have our three to six months fully funded emergency fund. I can't say enough how important it is to have the emergency fund. The impact of this plan on our lives has been substantial in just under a year!!

Michael (age 40)
and Laura (age 41) McCann
Security Systems Supervisor;
Stay-at-Home Mom

W hat an incredible two years it has been since my husband and I took part in Financial Peace University! Looking back now, we have no doubt that God's timing was perfect in presenting this practical financial wisdom to us at such a crucial period in our lives. At the time we started the plan, we had two car loans, student loans, medical bills, and over $20,000 in credit-card debt from frivolous college spending. While we easily made minimum payments, we knew we were only treading water, and any new expense or emergency would leave us drowning. Because of the principles learned through the plan, instead of increasing our standard of living at this time, we actually decreased our expenses by going to an all-cash system, and poured my entire paycheck into debt reduction.

At first, my husband was reluctant to do the plan, believing that we had everything under control. However, we were both hooked in no time! We actually got excited, talking and planning ways we could reduce our debt faster and how we could save more. As the bills were paid monthly, we kept a running total of our progress on the Debt Snowball. What a thrill it was to watch the amounts go lower and lower and to feel our burden being lifted!

What was so exciting about becoming financially free was not just that we were leaving a life of debt behind, but that we were planning awesome things for our future!

Here's the best part: As I write this testimonial, we are two months away from welcoming our first child into the world. By the time she arrives, we will be only a few months away from being free from debt. Before she was even conceived, she had a college fund started. And now, because two years ago we began paying off what has now amounted to over $50,000 in debt, I will be able to quit my job to be a full-time mommy! What an awesome blessing. We owe so much to The Total Money Makeover plan. Our new family thanks you.

> David (age 31)
> and Whitney (age 28) Scott
> Youth Minister/Director of
> Wings, a Mentoring
> Program for Pregnant Teens

We started out our lives with an SUV, student loans, credit card, a house, and a brand-new son (Wesley). Then we got a new wide-screen, high-definition TV and a surround-sound DVD system to go with it. We had acquired around $95,000 in debt! We had total "stuffitis" and no financial peace. We were completely NORMAL. Thanks to God's using Dave Ramsey in our lives and The Total Money Makeover, we are now changing.

At this point, we are at Baby Step Two. We have $1,000 in the bank, and we are working the Debt Snowball. Our first month on a budget was shaky and didn't work. The second month is better, so far, and we expect the third month to be smooth.

One of the best feelings about getting rid of our debt and being on a budget is to know where our money is going every month. We don't worry about spending too much. If the money is in the envelope, we can spend it. If the envelope is empty, we can't spend it. It's that simple.

Previously, we tried to get out of debt without a concrete plan. We weren't familiar with Dave's ideas. We were putting all our money toward debt and straining the family. I hadn't been letting my wife spend money on clothes or anything else before having a plan. Now that we are on a cash-flow plan, my wife gets excited because we have a clothing fund. The money stress is gone! Financial peace has arrived at the Keown household. We can enjoy life and get debt-free at the same time! We are looking forward to calling your show one day and yelling our victory. The Total Money Makeover is a mighty oracle.

*The Keown Family
Adam (age 24), Tobie (age 27),
and Wesley (age 5 months)
IT Director; Speech Therapist*

When I started The Total Money Makeover, I was at my wit's end. I was a young, self-employed, single mom with a three-year-old son. I also received no assistance from my ex-husband. A friend told me about "The Dave Way," and I asked if it would help me do a budget. She just laughed! She assured me it would help me do a budget and then some. I started working the plan with nine credit cards, a "fleeced" car, and other assorted loans totaling around $36,000. My mom and I decided to do the plan together.

By the end of thirteen weeks, I had paid off four credit cards totaling about $3,000. I had a garage sale along the way to help generate some extra income to put toward my Debt Snowball. I watched my money like a hawk! My young son even began to help me avoid my spending-addiction store of choice! He would whine when we got near it and be totally fine at any other store. I *guess he heard me lecturing myself and caught on. What's really cool is that my mom and I are working the buddy system and helping each other. My spending partner is now my saving partner!*

It's a few years later now, and I have whittled away over $10,000 in debt, paid off six creditors, and no longer have a leased car. My son is learning how to earn money, give money, and save money, too. We take a paid-for family vacation every year, and I match his savings through the year for his vacation spending. Although it will be a while before I'm debt-free, it is worth the wait. Thanks to Dave Ramsey's Total Money Makeover for helping me change my family tree!

Elizabeth Miller (age 27)
Full-Time student and Real
Estate Assistant

Before we began listening to Dave Ramsey, we were a single-paycheck family. We had no kids yet, but we did have debt—two car notes, seven credit cards, a line of revolving credit, and a moderate retirement. We bought a nice, 4,300-square-foot high-maintenance home for $250,000. What a mistake! The two of us didn't need that much house. There was no way to justify the payment or the "wasted" room. We kept trading cars to try to get a "BBD" (Bigger Better Deal), but the car-equity hole kept getting deeper or at least stayed the same. I'm not saying it's not okay to own some nice things, but the things owned us.

This was demonstrated in revolving debt and increasing marital discord. The "discussions" in our marriage were frequently over bills. We had no budget, no kids, and no plan. When our first child was born, we'd had it with increasing bills and housing costs. We had been an occasional listener for about two years, and I got tired of being that "doctor in debt" Dave talked about on his radio show. We started to work the plan. With the birth of our second child, we had a financial "rebirth."

We have paid off the cars. I paid cash for a nice used car for my wife and kids. I chose to drive an older car. We sold the $250,000 house for profit to an up-and-coming politician and bought a home for $133,000 and worked on it for two years. We have since bought our dream "fix-up" home and are *having a great time. We have put an addition on our "keeper" home and will still pay off the mortgage in ten years or less. It is now a joy to use money and not dread another "money discussion." Doing The Total Money Makeover taught us more about each other than any marriage counselor could. We now communicate openly and enjoy being a doctor out of debt, except for the mortgage.*

Jon (age 50)
and Dianna (age 37)
Parham
Physician;
High School Teacher

We had dug a little hole, and it was getting deeper and deeper. With a meager $3,000 in credit-card debt, we were financing a car and our furniture. It wasn't long before we were living paycheck to paycheck. We could pay a little over the minimum on our credit cards, but that was it. Looking back, the numbers weren't that big, but we were constantly stressed about money. And we had the most horrible money fights (they are the worst fights, aren't they?). What's really sad is that we had done it to ourselves.

Today, we are totally out of debt except for our mortgage and expect to pay it off in less than thirteen years. We have money—a fully funded emergency fund, a secure retirement plan, and a newfound confidence in our future. Perhaps most important is that we have discipline. The impact the plan has made on us is amazing. We tell everyone we know about Dave Ramsey and The Total Money Makeover plan. Our life is good; we have to make up stuff to fight about now! The plan worked for us, and it can work for anyone.

Ryman (age 33)
and Lesli (age 32) Peters
Pharmaceutical
Representative;
Administrative Support

When we started The Total Money Makeover plan, we'd only been married for three weeks and were polar opposites on money management. It was incredibly stressful to start out our marriage not being able to see how we were going to join our financial forces. We traded stress for prayer, and God delivered The Total Money Makeover plan!! What a huge blessing this has been for our personal finances!

In less than three years, we have dumped $54,614 (with $11,104 to go)! YAHOO! That ugly number consisted of IRS debt, credit cards, school loans, private school tuition, and a leased truck payment. We got mad, and then we got busy. We cut up our only two credit cards, established our budget, and had a garage sale and made $1,000 from it. We took on a two-month part-time job of throwing papers, sold a rental property, gave up the leased truck, and transferred our son from a private school to a small public school. My wife was able to quit work and stay home to manage our family affairs ten months after starting the plan.

Emotionally, I was shipwrecked before starting the plan and lay awake at nights wondering how I was going to support a new wife and son as I wanted and God expected. Debbie was just plain scared, scared that this new marriage wouldn't be so different from any other marriage in the area of money, that it was going to be a source of discontent for the rest of our days. Since The Total Money Makeover, I sleep soundly at night, and we both have a peace of knowing we are almost done serving our debt sentence. Spiritually, it feels incredibly wonderful knowing we are handling God's money God's way—total pleasure! Family-wise, our ten-year-old son saves money for all sorts of "wishes" and looks forward to rolling over his first $1,000 to a mutual fund so he can play golf after college and not have to have just a "job." This plan has changed our lives, our kids' lives, and the lives of our friends— FOREVER!

Joe (age 42)
and Debbie (age 31) Bynum
Self-Employed;
Stay-at-Home Mom

We first began to apply the principles of The Total Money Makeover a few summers ago. We thought we were in okay shape but had trouble getting a budget that really seemed to work for us. We have one consistent (salaried) income and a contractor's income (not so consistent). As with most families, one of us did the budget, and the other just moaned. The principles we learned from Dave Ramsey showed us how to "really" budget, but, most important, we began to talk about our money together and saw what we really owed. Beyond the budgeting, however, we learned and understood more on insurance and the Debt Snowball.

This information has made a significant change in our financial picture. We gained so much from Dave's teaching that we tag-team with another couple to pass the principles to others. This has helped us keep accountable as well as watching the positive change other families have made in their financial futures. We have made some great new friendships from being a part of The Total Money Makeover program. We highly recommend doing this plan . . . It will change your life!

Gary (age 47)
and Elaine (age 47) Bulmer
Contractor; Compliance
Specialist

While Kevin and I dated, we knew we would need help in the finance department. As an alumna of Dave Ramsey's teaching while single, I knew exactly what needed to happen. After a lot of discussion and becoming engaged, Kevin and I decided to work on The Total Money Makeover together. I already knew what a benefit the plan is, having gone through it, and I couldn't wait to see what it would do for both of us now.

By the time we married, we were very relieved and at "peace" that our wedding AND honeymoon were paid for completely with cash! We even came back with extra money from our honeymoon, which we were able to apply to our outstanding debt. What a great way to start our life together.

At this point in our lives, we have four outstanding debts left to tackle. With The Total Money Makeover, we will have two of those debts completely paid off in the next three months, a third paid off in twelve months, and then only my student loan left to pay off. Yes, we are walking in financial peace because of this plan!

> *Kevin (age 37)*
> *and Pam (age 34) Davis*
> *Forklift Operator; Child*
> *Development Coordinator*

The most valuable lesson I learned had nothing to do with the green paper that becomes such an idol to so many people; it was about trusting God.

Having been a single mom for fourteen years to two sons, now ages nineteen and twenty, I wanted more than anything in the world to make up to them what I felt they never got because they were not raised in a "married" household. Unfortunately, I used the credit card to soothe away some of the pain I saw on their faces today and tried not to think about the reality of what I was doing to my own future tomorrows. But tomorrow does come, and all of a sudden children are almost grown and gone, and I'm left with the finance charges and the balances—and the feeling that pulling out that credit card was a big mistake.

When I look back on my life, I wish I had learned many years ago to place my trust in God first above everything and everyone else, instead of putting that trust in plastic and the material things it provided. Since I began practicing Dave's principles, my two tithe checks are the most important checks I write every month. Those checks support my church, but, most important of all, they support my belief and faith in God, who will never change, who will never charge me interest, and, unlike a credit card will ALWAYS be there for me and provide for all my needs.

I strongly recommend that single parents follow The Total Money Makeover principles. It will change your spending habits, your thinking, and, most important, your heart.

> *Joyce Simmons (age 40-something)*
> *Single Mom*

My story closely parallels Dave's. I have been a real estate broker for over thirty years. In the late 1970s and early 1980s, having believed all of the garbage about using debt to create wealth, I ended up losing everything. I didn't file bank-ruptcy, but I did lose my marriage, and I have had to start all over again. God miraculously provided a new wife for me nearly five years ago, and we are working hard to finish cleaning up the financial mess from my past. Joyce encountered Financial Peace *several months ago at a local bookstore, and we have devoured its message and are adapting it to our lives.*

I never in my life had a savings account or a cash reserve of any kind, because I was so focused upon cleaning up debt that I wasn't sure I could jus-tify it. Now we have both a small savings and a cushion, and we are so excited about seeing how quickly God is going to help us become totally debt-free within just a few months. Our $184,000 mortgage balance will be the last to go, but we are already thinking about having a mortgage-burning party. Our motto for next year is "Debt-Free."

We are sick and tired of seeing God's children tied up in the world's eco-nomic system and unable to function in the calling of reaching our world effec-tively for Christ.

> *Roger (age 63)*
> *and Joyce (age 53) Swanson*
> *Real Estate*

A little over a year ago, I began listening to Dave on the radio, after years of my mother telling me I needed to tune in. I was very reluctant. I thought to myself that I didn't need another nut telling me that if I bought his materials I would be debt-free and set for life.

Listening the first day, I couldn't believe my ears. This guy was giving his stuff away for FREE? I could hear the passion in Dave's voice, and I knew he cared. I knew that he was real, genuine, and full of love for the Prince of Peace, Christ Jesus.

I am a Christian but wasn't living for Him. I had stopped most of the bad habits and had even given up long "friendships" in order to be better off. But I wasn't. No matter what I did, I never felt the void filled. When I heard Dave's personal testimony, it hit home. I thought I really knew Dave then. I guess that is why I am so passionate about his Total Money Makeover principles.

I encourage people just about daily to follow the plan. They always ask, "Dave talks about finance, right?" I tell them, "No, he talks about life and how it affects your finances." I am now so much happier. I am living for Jesus again, and I am closer than ever to having financial peace. In the past eighteen months, I have paid off nearly $25,000. Last year, I supplemented my base salary with over $10,000 of overtime pay. I have $800 dollars left to pay except for my house and can't wait to scream "I'm DEBT-FREE!"

Chris Howard (age 29)
Police Officer

I started listening to The Dave Ramsey Show about seven years ago. I kept hearing about all of the success stories and thinking this could never happen to us. We had too much debt.

We got married nine years ago and had our first baby two years later. I had every credit card from the mall you could have. When I felt depressed, I thought I could go and buy something new, and that would make me feel better. Collectors were calling all the time, even at work. I would spend my spare time looking at all of the bills and the balances and thinking How are we going to do this? At that time, our income was only about $25,000 per year. Our car payments were more than our rent. We got so far behind and still qualified for buying our first house. When we moved in, we didn't have any money saved. We barely had enough for closing costs. Things kept getting worse, and we got a foreclosure date on our house. The stress was really wearing on our relationship. Financial problems can tear you apart. One morning I walked out to go to work, opened the garage, and saw a tow truck ready to repossess my car. I would come home and the electricity would be off or the water would be cut off. I think that is when we hit our bottom. We filed bankruptcy. From there things could only get better; they couldn't get any worse.

We decided to start The Total Money Makeover plan. We started sitting down together to go over the bills and do our monthly budget. It really brought my husband and I closer together, and I didn't feel like I was the one responsible for all of the finances. We started putting money in savings. That was something we had never been able to do before. It was like we fell in love all over again. Last month, we paid off our bankruptcy eight months early. During that time we paid off about $45,000. We are finally "debt-free" and have money in savings. We have never been more in love than we are today. Thanks to The Total Money Makeover, it saved our money problems and our marriage!

Danny (age 32)
and Gina (age 30) Stricklin
Warehouse Supervisor;
Self-Employed

About eight years ago, I decided to open my own business. I was already a professional Volvo car technician, but I had never been self-employed. Due to poor spending habits, we already had a lot of consumer debt and a second mortgage on our house. As a result, I couldn't get a loan to start my business. So I started filling out the credit-card applications that showed up *in my mailbox every day. Soon I had $60,000 of unsecured credit at my disposal. I took out cash advances to lease a building, purchase equipment, and provide operating capital.*

Shortly thereafter, I started listening to Dave Ramsey and his Total Money Makeover principles. My wife, who had a successful wallpaper-hanging business, started listening too. Neither of us are rocket scientists, but we both quickly figured out that we were on very shaky ground with all of this debt. So we got mad! We decided that we would not take any income from the Volvo repair business, but use it all to retire debt. Within eighteen months, we had paid off $80,000 in business and personal debt, everything but our house. A short time later, we were able to establish a $10,000 emergency fund, at which time my wife retired (or hung it up, as we say in the wallpaper business).

We're still working The Total Money Makeover plan, and our home will be paid off within the next six years. With all of that debt retired, I thought we'd be ecstatic. We were happy, but the true emotion was peace, kind of like experiencing pain for a long time, and then it stops. We really did find financial peace.

Rod (age 53)
and Tori (age 51) Kruse
Volvo Repair Shop Owner;
Stay-at-Home Gardener and
Grandmother

Get your *personalized*

TOTAL MONEY MAKEOVER online!

There is NOTHING that matches what this amazing tool can do for you! It's incredible!

www.totalmoneymakeover.com/mytmmo

MyTMMO is a "virtual" personal finance fitness center. Create a personalized plan, track your results, store and modify personal information, work the plan and access thousands of question Dave has answered on The Dave Ramsey Show. Join and get your personalized plan today!

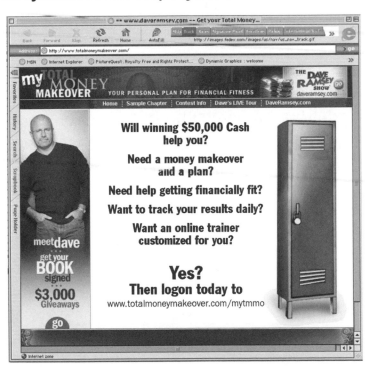

MAJOR COMPONENTS OF A
HEALTHY FINANCIAL PLAN

	Action Needed	Action Date
Written Cash-Flow Plan	_____	_____
Will and/or Estate Plan	_____	_____
Debt-Reduction Plan	_____	_____
Tax-Reduction Plan	_____	_____
Emergency Funding	_____	_____
Retirement Funding	_____	_____
College Funding	_____	_____
Charitable Giving	_____	_____
Teach My Children	_____	_____
Life Insurance	_____	_____
Health Insurance	_____	_____
Disability Insurance	_____	_____
Auto Insurance	_____	_____
Homeowners Insurance	_____	_____

I (We) _____, (a) responsible adult(s), do hereby promise to take the above-stated actions by the above-stated dates to financially secure the well-being of my (our) family and myself (ourselves).

Signed:_____ Date:_____
　　　　　(nerd, or saver)

Signed:_____ Date:_____
　　　　　(free spirit, or spender)

CONSUMER EQUITY SHEET

ITEM / DESCRIBE	VALUE	-	DEBT	=	EQUITY
Real Estate _____	_____		_____		_____
Real Estate _____	_____		_____		_____
Car _____	_____		_____		_____
Car _____	_____		_____		_____
Cash on Hand	_____		_____		_____
Checking Account	_____		_____		_____
Checking Account	_____		_____		_____
Savings Account	_____		_____		_____
Savings Account	_____		_____		_____
Money-Market Account	_____		_____		_____
Mutual Funds	_____		_____		_____
Retirement Plan	_____		_____		_____
Stocks or Bonds	_____		_____		_____
Cash Value (Insurance)	_____		_____		_____
Household Items	_____		_____		_____
Jewelry	_____		_____		_____
Antiques	_____		_____		_____
Boat	_____		_____		_____
Unsecured Debt (Neg)	_____		_____		_____
Credit Card Debt (Neg)	_____		_____		_____
Other _____	_____		_____		_____
Other _____	_____		_____		_____
Other _____	_____		_____		_____
TOTAL	_____		_____		_____

INCOME SOURCES

SOURCE	AMOUNT	PERIOD / DESCRIBE
Salary 1	_____	_____
Salary 2	_____	_____
Salary 3	_____	_____
Bonus	_____	_____
Self-Employment	_____	_____
Interest Income	_____	_____
Dividend Income	_____	_____
Royalty Income	_____	_____
Rents	_____	_____
Notes	_____	_____
Alimony	_____	_____
Child Support	_____	_____
AFDC	_____	_____
Unemployment	_____	_____
Social Security	_____	_____
Pension	_____	_____
Annuity	_____	_____
Disability Income	_____	_____
Cash Gifts	_____	_____
Trust Fund	_____	_____
Other _____	_____	_____
Other _____	_____	_____
Other _____	_____	_____
TOTAL	_____	_____

INSTRUCTIONS FOR MONTHLY CASH-FLOW PLAN

Every dollar of your income should be allocated to some category on this sheet. Money "left over" should be put back into a category even if you have to make up a new category. You are making the spending decisions ahead of time here. Almost every category (except debt) should have some dollar amount in it. Example: If you do not plan ahead to replace the furniture, when you do replace it, it will cause strain or borrowing, so go ahead and plan now by saving. I have actually had people tell me that they can do without clothing. Oh, come ON!! Be careful in your zeal to make the numbers work that you don't substitute the urgent for the important.

Fill in the amount for each subcategory under "Subtotal" and then the total for each main category under "Total." As you go through your first month, fill in the "Actually Spent" column with your real expenses or the saving you did for that area. If there is a substantial difference in the plan versus the reality, something has to give. You will either have to adjust the amount allocated to that area up and another down or you will have to better control your spending in that area.

"% of Take-Home Pay" is the percentage of take-home pay that category represents; for example, what percentage of your total take-home pay did you spend on "Housing"? We will then compare your percentages with those on the "Recommended Percentages sheet to determine if you need to consider adjusting your lifestyle.

An "*" beside an item means you should use the "envelope system."

The Emergency Fund should get ALL the savings until 3 to 6 months of expenses have been saved.

Note: Savings should be increased as you get closer to being debt free.

Hint: By saving early for Christmas and other gifts, you can get great buys and give better gifts for the same money.

- **You have 3 "Monthly Cash-Flow Plan" sheets beginning on the next page.**
- **Use these forms as your "zero"-based budget forms, which should be checked every few weeks.**
- **Make enough copies to do this for a one-year period in order to help you develop proper financial management habits.**

MONTHLY CASH-FLOW PLAN

Budgeted Item	Sub-total	TOTAL	Actually Spent	% of Take-Home Pay
CHARITABLE GIFTS	_____	_____	_____	_____
SAVING				
Emergency Fund	_____		_____	
Retirement Fund	_____		_____	
College Fund	_____	_____	_____	_____
HOUSING				
First Mortgage	_____			
Second Mortgage	_____			
Real-Estate Taxes	_____		_____	
Homeowners Ins.	_____		_____	
Repairs or Mn. Fee	_____		_____	
Replace Furniture	_____		_____	
Other _____	_____	_____	_____	_____
UTILITIES				
Electricity	_____		_____	
Water	_____		_____	
Gas	_____		_____	
Phone	_____		_____	
Trash	_____		_____	
Cable	_____	_____	_____	_____
*FOOD				
*Grocery	_____		_____	
*Restaurants	_____	_____	_____	_____
TRANSPORTATION				
Car Payment	_____		_____	
Car Payment	_____		_____	
*Gas and Oil	_____		_____	
*Repairs and Tires	_____		_____	
Car Insurance	_____		_____	
License and Taxes	_____		_____	
Car Replacement	_____	_____	_____	_____
PAGE 1 TOTAL		_____	_____	

MONTHLY CASH-FLOW PLAN

Budgeted Item	Sub-total	TOTAL	Actually Spent	% of Take-Home Pay
*CLOTHING				
*Children	_____		_____	
*Adults	_____		_____	
*Cleaning/Laundry	_____	_____	_____	_____
MEDICAL/HEALTH				
Disability Insurance	_____		_____	
Health Insurance	_____		_____	
Doctor Bills	_____		_____	
Dentist	_____		_____	
Optometrist	_____		_____	
Drugs	_____	_____	_____	_____
PERSONAL				
Life Insurance	_____		_____	
Child Care	_____		_____	
*Baby-sitter	_____		_____	
*Toiletries	_____		_____	
*Cosmetics	_____		_____	
*Hair Care	_____		_____	
Education/Adult	_____		_____	
School Tuition	_____		_____	
School Supplies	_____		_____	
Child Support	_____		_____	
Alimony	_____		_____	
Subscriptions	_____		_____	
Organization Dues	_____		_____	
Gifts (incl. Christmas)	_____		_____	
Miscellaneous	_____		_____	
*BLOW $$	_____	_____	_____	_____
PAGE 2 TOTAL		_____		

MONTHLY CASH-FLOW PLAN

Budgeted Item	Sub-total	TOTAL	Actually Spent	% of Take-Home Pay
RECREATION				
*Entertainment	_____		_____	
Vacation	_____	_____	_____	_____
DEBTS (Hopefully -0-)				
Visa 1	_____		_____	
Visa 2	_____		_____	
MasterCard 1	_____		_____	
MasterCard 2	_____		_____	
American Express	_____		_____	
Discover Card	_____		_____	
Gas Card 1	_____		_____	
Gas Card 2	_____		_____	
Dept. Store Card 1	_____		_____	
Dept. Store Card 2	_____		_____	
Finance Co. 1	_____		_____	
Finance Co. 2	_____		_____	
Credit Line	_____		_____	
Student Loan 1	_____		_____	
Student Loan 2	_____		_____	
Other _____	_____		_____	
Other _____	_____		_____	
Other _____	_____		_____	
Other _____	_____		_____	
Other _____	_____	_____	_____	_____
PAGE 3 TOTAL		_____	_____	
PAGE 2 TOTAL		_____	_____	
PAGE 1 TOTAL		_____	_____	
GRAND TOTAL		_____	_____	
TOTAL HOUSEHOLD INCOME		_____		
		ZERO		

RECOMMENDED PERCENTAGES

I have used a compilation of several sources and my own experience to derive the suggested percentage guidelines. However, these are only recommended percentages and will change dramatically if you have a very high or very low income. For instance, if you have a very low income, your necessities percentages will be high. If you have a high income, your necessities will be a lower percentage of income, and hopefully savings (not debt) will be higher than recommended.

ITEM	ACTUAL %	RECOMMENDED %
CHARITABLE GIFTS	_____	10–15%
SAVING	_____	5–10%
HOUSING	_____	25–35%
UTILITIES	_____	5–10%
FOOD	_____	5–15%
TRANSPORTATION	_____	10–15%
CLOTHING	_____	2–7%
MEDICAL/HEALTH	_____	5–10%
PERSONAL	_____	5–10%
RECREATION	_____	5–10%
DEBTS	_____	5–10%

INSTRUCTIONS FOR ALLOCATED-SPENDING PLAN

This sheet is where all your work thus far starts giving you some peace. You will implement your "Monthly Cash Flow Plan" from theory into your life by using the "Allocated Spending Plan." Note: If you have an irregular income, such as self-employment or commissions, you should use the "Irregular Income Planning" sheet, after reviewing your Allocated-Spending Plan.

There are four columns to distribute as many as four different incomes within one month. Each column is one pay period. If you are a one-income household, and you get paid two times per month, then you will only use two columns. If both of you work, and one is paid weekly and the other every two weeks, add the two paychecks together on the weeks you both get a paycheck, while just listing the one paycheck on the other two. Date the pay-period columns, then enter the income for that period. As you allocate your paycheck to an item, put the remaining total balance to the right of the slash. Income for period 3/1 in our example is $1,000, and we are allocating $100 to Charitable Giving, leaving $900 to the right of the slash in that same column. Some bills will come out of each pay period and some only on selected pay periods. As an example, you may take "Car Gas" out of every paycheck, but pay the electric bill from period 2. You already pay some bills or payments out of designated checks, only now you pay all things from designated checks.

The whole point to this sheet, which is the culmination of all your monthly planning, is to allocate or "spend" your whole paycheck before you get paid. I don't care where you allocate your money, but allocate all of it before you get your check. Now all the tense, crisislike symptoms have been removed, because you planned. No more management by crisis or impulse. Those who tend to be impulsive should just allocate more to the "Blow" category. At least you are now doing it on purpose and not by default. The last blank that you make an entry in should have a "0" to the right of the slash, showing you have allocated your whole check.

An "*" beside an item means you should use the "envelope system."

Emergency Fund gets ALL the savings until 3 to 6 months of expenses have been saved.

SAMPLE ALLOCATED SPENDING PLAN

PAY PERIOD:	3/1			
ITEM				
INCOME	1,000			
CHARITABLE GIFTS	100/900	__/__	__/__	__/__
SAVING				
Emergency Fund(1)	50/850	__/__	__/__	__/__
Retirement Fund	__/__	__/__	__/__	__/__
College Fund	__/__	__/__	__/__	__/__
HOUSING				
First Mortgage	725/125	__/__	__/__	__/__

ALLOCATED-SPENDING PLAN

PAY PERIOD: _____ _____ _____ _____

ITEM

INCOME   _____ _____ _____ _____

CHARITABLE GIFTS   ___/___ ___/___ ___/___ ___/___

SAVING

    Emergency Fund   ___/___ ___/___ ___/___ ___/___

    Retirement Fund   ___/___ ___/___ ___/___ ___/___

    College Fund   ___/___ ___/___ ___/___ ___/___

HOUSING

    First Mortgage   ___/___ ___/___ ___/___ ___/___

    Second Mortgage   ___/___ ___/___ ___/___ ___/___

    Real-Estate Taxes   ___/___ ___/___ ___/___ ___/___

    Homeowners Ins.   ___/___ ___/___ ___/___ ___/___

    Repairs or Mn. Fees   ___/___ ___/___ ___/___ ___/___

    Replace Furniture   ___/___ ___/___ ___/___ ___/___

    Other _____   ___/___ ___/___ ___/___ ___/___

UTILITIES

    Electricity   ___/___ ___/___ ___/___ ___/___

    Water   ___/___ ___/___ ___/___ ___/___

    Gas   ___/___ ___/___ ___/___ ___/___

    Phone   ___/___ ___/___ ___/___ ___/___

    Trash   ___/___ ___/___ ___/___ ___/___

    Cable   ___/___ ___/___ ___/___ ___/___

*FOOD

    *Grocery   ___/___ ___/___ ___/___ ___/___

    *Restaurants   ___/___ ___/___ ___/___ ___/___

ALLOCATED-SPENDING PLAN

TRANSPORTATION
    Car Payment _____/_____   _____/_____   _____/_____   _____/_____
    Car Payment _____/_____   _____/_____   _____/_____   _____/_____
    *Gas and Oil _____/_____   _____/_____   _____/_____   _____/_____
    *Repairs and Tires _____/_____   _____/_____   _____/_____   _____/_____
    Car Insurance _____/_____   _____/_____   _____/_____   _____/_____
    License and Taxes _____/_____   _____/_____   _____/_____   _____/_____
    Car Replacement _____/_____   _____/_____   _____/_____   _____/_____

*CLOTHING
    *Children _____/_____   _____/_____   _____/_____   _____/_____
    *Adults _____/_____   _____/_____   _____/_____   _____/_____
    *Cleaning/Laundry _____/_____   _____/_____   _____/_____   _____/_____

MEDICAL/HEALTH
    Disability Insurance _____/_____   _____/_____   _____/_____   _____/_____
    Health Insurance _____/_____   _____/_____   _____/_____   _____/_____
    Doctor _____/_____   _____/_____   _____/_____   _____/_____
    Dentist _____/_____   _____/_____   _____/_____   _____/_____
    Optometrist _____/_____   _____/_____   _____/_____   _____/_____
    Drugs _____/_____   _____/_____   _____/_____   _____/_____

PERSONAL
    Life Insurance _____/_____   _____/_____   _____/_____   _____/_____
    Child Care _____/_____   _____/_____   _____/_____   _____/_____
    *Baby-sitter _____/_____   _____/_____   _____/_____   _____/_____
    *Toiletries _____/_____   _____/_____   _____/_____   _____/_____
    *Cosmetics _____/_____   _____/_____   _____/_____   _____/_____
    *Hair Care _____/_____   _____/_____   _____/_____   _____/_____
    Education/Adult _____/_____   _____/_____   _____/_____   _____/_____
    School Tuition _____/_____   _____/_____   _____/_____   _____/_____
    School Supplies _____/_____   _____/_____   _____/_____   _____/_____
    Child Support _____/_____   _____/_____   _____/_____   _____/_____

ALLOCATED-SPENDING PLAN

Alimony ___/___ ___/___ ___/___ ___/___

Subscriptions ___/___ ___/___ ___/___ ___/___

Organization Dues ___/___ ___/___ ___/___ ___/___

Gifts (incl.Christmas) ___/___ ___/___ ___/___ ___/___

Miscellaneous ___/___ ___/___ ___/___ ___/___

*BLOW $$ ___/___ ___/___ ___/___ ___/___

RECREATION

   *Entertainment ___/___ ___/___ ___/___ ___/___

Vacation ___/___ ___/___ ___/___ ___/___

DEBTS (Hopefully -0-)

Visa 1 ___/___ ___/___ ___/___ ___/___

Visa 2 ___/___ ___/___ ___/___ ___/___

MasterCard 1 ___/___ ___/___ ___/___ ___/___

MasterCard 2 ___/___ ___/___ ___/___ ___/___

American Express ___/___ ___/___ ___/___ ___/___

Discover Card ___/___ ___/___ ___/___ ___/___

Gas Card 1 ___/___ ___/___ ___/___ ___/___

Gas Card 2 ___/___ ___/___ ___/___ ___/___

Dept. Store Card 1 ___/___ ___/___ ___/___ ___/___

Dept. Store Card 2 ___/___ ___/___ ___/___ ___/___

Finance Co. 1 ___/___ ___/___ ___/___ ___/___

Finance Co. 2 ___/___ ___/___ ___/___ ___/___

Credit Line ___/___ ___/___ ___/___ ___/___

Student Loan 1 ___/___ ___/___ ___/___ ___/___

Student Loan 2 ___/___ ___/___ ___/___ ___/___

Other _____ ___/___ ___/___ ___/___ ___/___

Other _____ ___/___ ___/___ ___/___ ___/___

Other _____ ___/___ ___/___ ___/___ ___/___

Other _____ ___/___ ___/___ ___/___ ___/___

Other _____ ___/___ ___/___ ___/___ ___/___

IRREGULAR-INCOME PLANNING

Many of us have irregular incomes. If you are self-employed or work on commission or royalties, then planning your expenses is difficult, since you cannot always predict your income. You should still do all the sheets except the Allocated Spending Plan. The Monthly Cash-Flow Plan will tell you what you have to earn monthly to survive or prosper, and those real numbers are very good for goal setting.

What you must do is take the items on the Monthly Cash-Flow Plan and prioritize them by importance. I repeat: by importance, not urgency. You should ask yourself, "If I only have enough money to pay one thing, what would that be?" Then ask, "If I only have enough money to pay one more thing, what would that be?" Move this way through the list. Now be prepared to stand your ground because things have a way of seeming important that are only urgent. Saving should be a high priority!

The third column, "Cumulative Amount," is the total of all amounts above that item. So, if you get a $2,000 check, you can see how far down your priority list you can go.

Item	*Amount*	*Cumulative Amount*
_____	_____	_____
_____	_____	_____
_____	_____	_____
_____	_____	_____
_____	_____	_____
_____	_____	_____
_____	_____	_____
_____	_____	_____
_____	_____	_____

IRREGULAR-INCOME PLANNING

Item	Amount	Cumulative Amount
_____	_____	_____
_____	_____	_____
_____	_____	_____
_____	_____	_____
_____	_____	_____
_____	_____	_____
_____	_____	_____
_____	_____	_____
_____	_____	_____
_____	_____	_____
_____	_____	_____
_____	_____	_____
_____	_____	_____
_____	_____	_____
_____	_____	_____
_____	_____	_____

BREAKDOWN OF SAVINGS

After your emergency fund is fully funded, you can save for certain items like furniture, car replacement, home maintenance, or clothes, and your savings balance will grow. This sheet is designed to remind you that all of that money is committed to something, not just a Hawaiian vacation on impulse because you are now "rich." Keep up with your breakdown of savings monthly for one quarter at a time.

ITEM	BALANCE BY MONTH:			
Emergency Fund (1)	$1000			
Emergency Fund (2)	3–6 months			
Retirement Fund				
College Fund				
Real-Estate Taxes				
Homeowners Insurance				
Repairs or Mn. Fee				
Replace Furniture				
Car Insurance				
Car Replacement				
Disability Insurance				
Health Insurance				
Doctor				
Dentist				
Optometrist				
Life Insurance				
School Tuition				
School Supplies				
Gifts (incl. Christmas)				
Vacation				
Other _____				
Other _____				
TOTAL				

THE DEBT SNOWBALL

List your debts in order with the smallest payoff or balance first. Do not be concerned with interest rates or terms unless two debts have similar payoffs, then list the higher-interest-rate debt first. Paying the little debts off first gives you quick feedback, and you are more likely to stay with the plan.

Redo this sheet each time you pay off a debt, so you can see how close you are getting to freedom. Keep the old sheets to wallpaper the bathroom in your new debt-free house. The "New Payment" is found by adding all the payments on the debts listed above that item to the payment you are working on, so you have compounding payments, which will get you out of debt very quickly. "Payments Remaining" is the number of payments remaining on that debt when you get down the snowball to that item. "Cumulative Payments" is the total payments needed, including the snowball, to pay off that item. In other words, this is your running total for "Payments Remaining."

COUNTDOWN TO FREEDOM!!

Date:_____

Item	Total Payoff	Minimum Payment	New Payment	Payments Remaining	Cumulative Payments
_____	_____	_____	_____	_____	_____
_____	_____	_____	_____	_____	_____
_____	_____	_____	_____	_____	_____
_____	_____	_____	_____	_____	_____
_____	_____	_____	_____	_____	_____
_____	_____	_____	_____	_____	_____
_____	_____	_____	_____	_____	_____
_____	_____	_____	_____	_____	_____
_____	_____	_____	_____	_____	_____
_____	_____	_____	_____	_____	_____
_____	_____	_____	_____	_____	_____
_____	_____	_____	_____	_____	_____

THE DEBT SNOWBALL

Item	Total Payoff	Minimum Payment	New Payment	Payments Remaining	Cumulative Payments
_____	_____	_____	_____	_____	_____
_____	_____	_____	_____	_____	_____
_____	_____	_____	_____	_____	_____
_____	_____	_____	_____	_____	_____
_____	_____	_____	_____	_____	_____
_____	_____	_____	_____	_____	_____
_____	_____	_____	_____	_____	_____
_____	_____	_____	_____	_____	_____
_____	_____	_____	_____	_____	_____
_____	_____	_____	_____	_____	_____
_____	_____	_____	_____	_____	_____
_____	_____	_____	_____	_____	_____
_____	_____	_____	_____	_____	_____
_____	_____	_____	_____	_____	_____
_____	_____	_____	_____	_____	_____
_____	_____	_____	_____	_____	_____
_____	_____	_____	_____	_____	_____
_____	_____	_____	_____	_____	_____
_____	_____	_____	_____	_____	_____
_____	_____	_____	_____	_____	_____
_____	_____	_____	_____	_____	_____
_____	_____	_____	_____	_____	_____
_____	_____	_____	_____	_____	_____
_____	_____	_____	_____	_____	_____
_____	_____	_____	_____	_____	_____

PRO RATA DEBTS

If you cannot pay your creditors what they request, you should treat them all fairly and the same. You should pay even the ones who are not jerks, and pay everyone as much as you can. Many creditors will accept a written plan and cut special deals with you as long as you are communicating, maybe even over-communicating, and sending them something. We have had clients use this even when sending only $2 payments and survive for literally years.

Pro Rata means "their share": the percent of total debt each creditor represents. That will determine how much you send them. Then, you send the check with a budget and this sheet attached each month, even if the creditor says they will not accept it.

Item	Total Payoff	Total Debt	=Percent	Disposable X Income	New = Payments
_____	_____	/_____	=._____	X_____	=_____
_____	_____	/_____	=._____	X_____	=_____
_____	_____	/_____	=._____	X_____	=_____
_____	_____	/_____	=._____	X_____	=_____
_____	_____	/_____	=._____	X_____	=_____
_____	_____	/_____	=._____	X_____	=_____
_____	_____	/_____	=._____	X_____	=_____
_____	_____	/_____	=._____	X_____	=_____
_____	_____	/_____	=._____	X_____	=_____
_____	_____	/_____	=._____	X_____	=_____
_____	_____	/_____	=._____	X_____	=_____
_____	_____	/_____	=._____	X_____	=_____
_____	_____	/_____	=._____	X_____	=_____
_____	_____	/_____	=._____	X_____	=_____
_____	_____	/_____	=._____	X_____	=_____
_____	_____	/_____	=._____	X_____	=_____

"TRAINING TOMORROW'S MILLIONAIRES... YOUR KIDS!"

LIFE LESSONS
with Junior

This series will teach basic principles about money and, yes, life. From working and saving to giving and spending, these wonderful stories will teach real life 'stuff' and the stories are so fun, your children won't even know they're learning!

FINANCIAL PEACE JR.
Training Tomorrow's Millionaires

This unique collection of teaching tools will help create healthy money management habits in your children that will last a lifetime.

order now at www.daveramsey.com or 888-22-PEACE